Library of
Davidson College

Jobs in a
Sustainable Economy

Michael Renner

Worldwatch Paper 104
September 1991

Sections of this paper may be reproduced in magazines and newspapers with acknowledgment to the Worldwatch Institute. The views expressed are those of the author and do not necessarily represent those of the Worldwatch Institute and its directors, officers, or staff, or of funding organizations.

© Worldwatch Institute, 1991
Library of Congress Catalog Number 91-066301

ISBN 1-878071-05-X

Printed on recycled paper

Table of Contents

A False Dilemma 5

Toward a Sustainable Economy 8

Pollution Abatement and Control 17

Energy Efficiency and Renewables.......................................24

Railroads versus Highways...29

Recycling Materials, Retaining Jobs 33

Sustainable Forestry: From Logging to Stewardship............36

Making the Transition 41

Notes 48

A False Dilemma

"Save a Logger. Kill an Owl," exhorts a bumper sticker popular in the U.S. Pacific Northwest, where timber companies have suggested that measures to protect an endangered species from extinction will cost the jobs of tens of thousands of loggers. As the provocative slogan suggests, the northern spotted owl has become a symbol of the seemingly intractable conflict between jobs and environmental protection—and of the larger tensions between the health of the economy and that of the natural world on which the economy ultimately depends.

The ever-changing interplay between jobs and the environment is far too complex to be reduced to any bumper sticker, but this one is particularly pernicious. While there are undoubtedly cases in which new environmental laws throw individual workers out of their jobs, such cases are in fact rare, and often counterbalanced by jobs created in pollution control or in entirely new fields. The bottom line is that a more environmentally sustainable economy is compatible with full and rewarding employment. In a stable ecosystem, the loggers and their children will be far more protected—not only from the loss of their jobs but from massive threats to life and health.

For centuries, the world's economies have depended on the ability to deplete one non-renewable source after another, to draw down the regenerative capacity of many living systems, and to treat the world's waterways and atmosphere as if they were free receptacles for the disposal of pollution. But the day of reckoning has arrived, and major structural adjustments are inevitable as the world faces up to the unprecedented environmental threats now looming. If the global econo-

---

I am grateful to Ann Misch for her invaluable research support, Greg Bischak and my colleagues at Worldwatch for their review comments, and Mark Cohen, Holger Eisl, Mike Frisch, and Anita Glazer Sadun for many helpful suggestions.

my is to be protected from the kind of chaos that ecological decline can produce, it will need to move inexorably—and in some cases sharply—toward a more sustainable relationship with the natural resource base that underpins it. The nature and number of jobs in the economy will be deeply affected by this transition.

What it will take is clear: renewable energy sources will have to begin replacing oil and coal, not only to bring air pollution under control but to slow the global warming that poses a mounting threat to all life. The tragedy of declining tree cover and diminishing biodiversity on every continent will have to be reversed, even in the face of a rapidly expanding world population. And less materials-intensive manufacturing and processing industries will need to be developed.

Less damaging ways of producing, consuming, and disposing of goods are fully consistent with the goal of full employment because they tend to be far more labor-intensive. A well-paid, rewarding job does not have to be polluting; nor does it have to be created at the expense of someone else's job.

As economic changes unfold, a host of job opportunities will emerge. Many existing occupations—such as home insulation contracting—are likely to grow, while entirely new professions—such as wind farm surveying—are likely to be created. Among particular industries and communities, there will of course be short-term winners and losers. Highway construction, cattle ranching, and high-sulfur coal mining will likely decline. Rail car assembly, solar collector manufacturing, and materials recycling will boom.

The challenge is to create millions of new jobs in a world already plagued by massive unemployment. The task is particularly difficult in developing countries where increases in employment have not kept up with unprecedented rates of population growth in recent years. In the Third World as a whole, hundreds of millions of people lack adequate jobs, and unemployment rates run as high as 20 to 30 percent. Even in the industrial countries that have led the assault on the environment and are now faced with leading the rescue, official unemployment figures have grown from 3 percent in the early sixties to 7.5 percent in the late eighties. In a world in which a billion people will be added to the population in the next 12 years, in which industries are in constant flux, and in which international shifts in the jobs market occur quickly and unpredictably, the challenge of gainfully employing everyone who wants to work can only mount.[1]

Unfortunately, conventional approaches to economic development, which produce enormous amounts of pollution and consume huge quantities of energy and materials in the pursuit of ever higher rates of economic growth, often fail to deliver one of the most important products of any economy: sufficient jobs. The dilemma is that achieving anything near full employment would, under such circumstances, require even higher—and utterly unsustainable—levels of growth. This dilemma is particularly severe for developing countries, since the resource-intensive or extractive industries on which they depend are likely to decline.[2]

This is one problem that cannot simply be "left to the market," particularly since there are a host of existing government policies that both encourage pollution and discourage job creation. By shifting the tax burden away from labor and toward capital and energy, job creation can be spurred. And by creating community rehabilitation and worker training programs, the burden of the transition can be eased. Just as governments have helped to create the economic and environmental problems that societies are now faced with, so are they responsible for helping to pave the way for the transition.

The sooner we embrace the principles of sustainability as an essential goal of public policy, the less traumatic the transition will be. An early decision to alter or abandon environmentally destructive practices is likely to cause fewer economic problems or job losses than a reactive policy. Although the short-term costs of redesigning products and production technologies can be high, delaying a response until it is dictated by sheer ecological necessity would be even more costly.

The most difficult challenge ahead is political: to persuade companies and unions to accept the fact that what is good for the spotted owl is often in the long run interest of workers as well. However, unions are reluctant to abandon the postwar growth pact that brought steadily rising wages for their members and a greater role in decision-making for union representatives. Corporate threats to close down factories often succeed in mobilizing workers and communities to oppose regulatory policies—even though these communities would be among the first to benefit from their implementation. This "job blackmail" makes it harder to forge coalitions between the labor and environmental movements. But the rise of endemic unemployment, and the erosion of real wages since the seventies, have compelled labor leaders to take a new look at their interests.[3]

Many of those leaders now understand that ecological health and economic well-being are inseparable. On one hand, the economy cannot depend forever on depleting natural resources, degrading ecosystems, and rendering large areas unfit for habitation. On the other, it is hard to see how ecological sustainability can be achieved in the absence of economic well-being. As a report by the United Steelworkers of America put it: "In the long run, the real choice is not jobs or environment. It's both or neither. What kind of jobs will be possible in a world of depleted resources, poisoned water and foul air, a world where ozone depletion and greenhouse warming make it difficult even to survive?"[4]

Toward a Sustainable Economy

If environmental degradation is not to become irreversible, fundamental changes in the way products are produced, used, and disposed of are unavoidable. A sustainable society will have to give greater emphasis to conservation and efficiency, rely more on renewable energy, and extract nominally renewable resources only to the degree that they can regenerate themselves. It will need to minimize waste, maximize reuse and recycling, avoid the use of hazardous materials, and preserve biodiversity. And it will need to develop more environmentally benign production

> "The question is not whether economies will change as a result of environmental concerns, but in what directions they will evolve, what the job prospects will be, and how governments can guide and smooth the process."

technologies, and design products to be more durable and repairable.

As progress is made toward these goals, the worst environmental offenders, including the oil, coal, chemical, and motor vehicle industries, will shrink; some may eventually disappear altogether. In their place, new industries will emerge. Just as automobiles, synthetic chemistry, and throw-away products characterized life during much of the 20th century, so will the features of an environmentally sustainable economy—energy-efficient appliances and homes, short commutes, bike paths, solar power plants, and recycling centers—reshape life in the 21st.

While such dramatic changes may be hard to imagine, they have ample historical precedent; modern economies are anything but static. From the Industrial Revolution onward, economic activity and employment have continually shifted —from agriculture to manufacturing to services. In the countries of the Organisation for Economic Co-operation and Development (OECD), industrial employment gradually declined from 35 to 30 percent of total employment between 1960 and 1988, and agricultural jobs fell from 22 to 8 percent. During the same period, service jobs climbed from 43 to 62 percent. The composition of industry itself is continuing to change: in the industrialized countries, traditional industries such as textiles, iron and steel, and metals processing are declining, while electronics, telecommunications, and biotechnology are gaining. The question is not whether economies will change as a result of environmental concerns, but in what directions they will evolve, what the job prospects will be, and how governments can guide and smooth the process.[5]

Conventional economic theory holds that a dynamic economy sheds jobs in mature industries but creates sufficient new employment in emerging industries. Increasing labor productivity—the ability to make a product with fewer employees—is generally not seen as a problem, but as a desirable outcome. Overall, the ranks of the workforce have grown because the total volume of goods and services produced has expanded dramatically, offsetting the labor-saving effects of automation. Yet, while the microelectronics revolution has spawned whole new industries, it has also reduced the need for labor throughout the economy. Since the seventies, virtually every country has been struggling with pervasive structural unemployment—and with the unsettling discovery that economic growth is no longer always accompanied by a commensurate increase in the number of jobs. (See Figure 1.)[6]

The pattern of economic development followed by the United States and other industrial economies after World War II set the stage for both the unemployment and environmental crises. In his 1976 book, *The Poverty of Power*, Barry Commoner summarized: "The amount of energy and

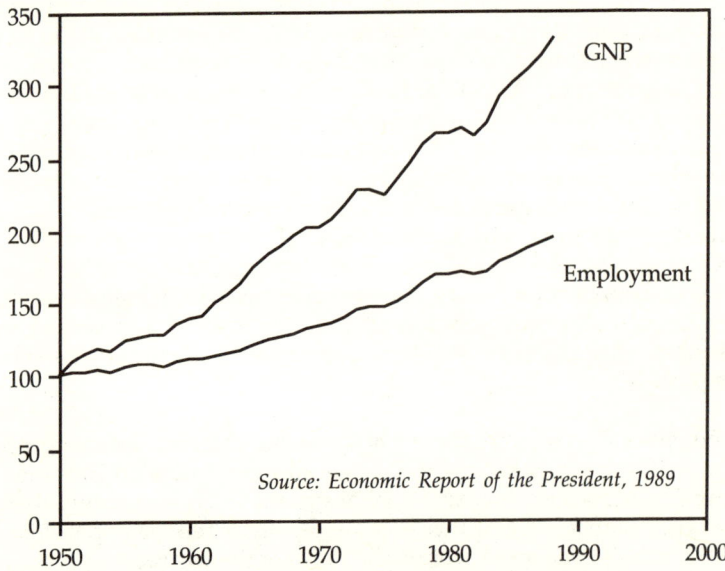

Figure 1: Rise in GNP and Civilian Employment in the U.S.: 1950–88

> "Polluting industries are at best a marginal—
> and now shrinking—source of jobs."

capital needed to accomplish the same task has increased; the amount of labor used to produce the same output has decreased; the impact on the environment has worsened." The efficiency of industrial energy use has increased 30 percent since 1973, but capital and energy are being substituted for human labor, which is in chronic surplus. Having millions of people out of work is considered normal. What seems to make good business sense from the corporate point of view poses a serious dilemma for society as a whole. By shedding workers, companies can cut their costs, but if those laid off fail to find new jobs, the burden of support—and of coping with the social consequences—falls on society.[7]

The U.S. economy epitomizes these trends. Between 1950 and 1986, the output of the U.S. manufacturing sector, adjusted for inflation, more than tripled. But while the amount of energy used also nearly tripled and the quantity of capital (measured by the value of machinery and buildings) increased four-fold, the input of labor (as measured by the total number of hours worked) rose by only about one third. As a result, the productivities of these inputs—the relative amounts required to produce a particular product—diverged dramatically. While capital productivity remained almost unchanged until 1974 and then fell by almost 20 percent over the next decade, labor productivity increased 2.5-fold. (See Figure 2.)[8]

Five manufacturing industries—primary metals, paper, oil refining, chemicals, and stone, clay, and glass—are notable for their high use of energy and capital on one hand, and low labor needs on the other. (See Table 1.) These are also, by far, the biggest polluters. Among them, they account for 80 to 85 percent of both energy use and toxics releases within the U.S. manufacturing sector—but for only 17 percent of its employment. They use 21 percent of the energy consumed in the U.S. economy as a whole, but provide only 3 percent of the jobs. (See Table 2.) In the transportation, electric utility, and mining industries, similarly, high levels of energy consumption and pollution are accompanied by low levels of employment.[9]

Polluting industries are at best a marginal—and now shrinking—source

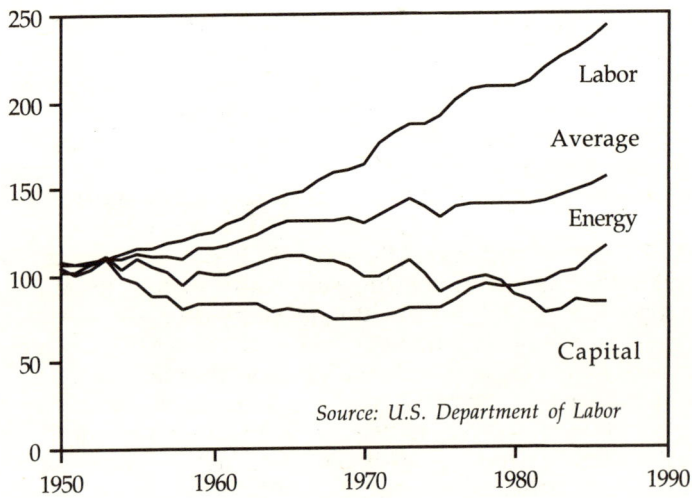

Figure 2. U. S. Manufacturing: Capital, Labor, and Energy Productivities, 1950–86

of jobs. In most countries, the energy and chemical industries each account for less than 3 percent of total employment. Even in the absence of environmental policies, many of these jobs are disappearing. For example, a quarter of all U.S. refining jobs were eliminated between 1982 and 1990. And, despite rising production, U.S. coal mining jobs fell sharply during the eighties, from 250,000 to 150,000. With further gains in labor productivity, additional losses are expected in the nineties. Similar patterns are found in Europe.[10]

Throughout the world, industrial economies and employment are con-

Table 1. Labor, Capital, and Energy Productivities in Manufacturing and Mining, United States, 1987/88[1]

Industry	Inputs Needed to Generate $1,000 of Value-Added:		
	Labor	Capital	Energy
	(Hours)	(Dollars of Assets[2])	(Million BTUs)
ALL MANUFACTURING	21	791	12.1
Refining & Coal Products	9	2,670	127.0
Primary Metal	24	1,581	45.9
Paper	19	1,448	36.7
Stone, Clay & Glass	25	1,066	29.5
Chemicals	8	1,039	22.4
Lumber & Wood Products	40	805	13.0
Textiles	46	914	10.8
Food Products	17	665	7.6
Rubber & Misc. Plastics	29	813	5.6
Fabricated Metal	29	704	4.4
Leather	47	318	3.3
Furniture & Fixtures	40	438	3.1
Transportation Equipment	18	649	2.4
Electrical Machinery	20	695	2.2
Non-Electrical Machinery	20	677	2.0
Tobacco	4	427	1.4
Printing & Publishing	17	507	1.3
Instruments	14	504	1.3
Apparel	50	243	1.3
ALL MINING	8	760	17.7
Nonmetallic Minerals	19	1,830	33.1
Metal Mining	15	2,970	25.8
Oil & Gas Extraction	5	340	17.3
Coal Mining	15	1,550	9.6

[1]Labor and Capital data are for 1987, energy data for 1988. [2]Gross value of depreciable assets. Sources: See footnote 9.

Table 2. Energy Use, Pollution, and Employment by Economic Activity, United States, 1987/88.

Industry	GDP	Employment	Energy Use	Toxics Release
	(Percent of all Manufacturing)			
Refining & Coal Products	3.9	.8	31.2	3.7
Chemicals	9.0	5.5	21.2	58.4
Primary Metal	4.3	4.0	14.0	12.5
Paper	4.6	3.6	11.5	13.6
Food Products	8.7	8.4	4.8	1.4
Stone, Clay & Glass	3.2	3.1	4.7	.5
Lumber & Wood Products	3.2	3.9	2.0	.2
Transportation Equipment	5.8	10.6	1.7	1.6
Fabricated Metal	7.1	7.4	1.7	1.5
Non-Electrical Machinery	9.5	10.7	1.4	.4
Electrical Machinery	10.0	10.7	1.1	1.4
Printing & Publishing	6.8	8.0	.6	.3
Other Manufacturing[1]	23.8	23.3	4.1	4.2
ALL MANUFACTURING	100.0	100.0	100.0	100.0

[1] Tobacco, textiles, apparel, furniture and fixtures, rubber and miscellaneous plastics, instruments, leather, and miscellaneous manufacturing.

Sources: Worldwatch Institute, compiled and calculated from U.S. Department of Commerce, Bureau of the Census, *1987 Census of Manufactures* and *1987 Census of Mineral Industries* (Washington, D.C.: U.S. Government Printing Office, 1990); U.S. Department of Energy, Energy Information Administration, *Manufacturing Energy Consumption Survey: Consumption of Energy 1988* (Washington, D.C.: GPO, May 1991); Environmental Protection Agency, *The Toxics Release Inventory* (Washington, D.C.: GPO, June 1989).

tinuing to shift from manufacturing to the service sectors, which consume little energy and are still relatively labor-intensive. Where the bulk of bread-winners were once farmers and factory workers, they are now computer operators, administrators, accountants, and clerks. Relatively

> "Until manufacturers change their fundamental methods of production, industrial pollution will continue to cripple both people and the environment."

few work any longer in the heavy industries that generate most of the pollution. But services can never entirely replace manufacturing, and the exodus of workers from manufacturing won't reduce the need for manufactured products. The demand for such products will continue, but until manufacturers change their fundamental methods of production, industrial pollution will continue to cripple both people and the environment.[11]

The initial response of many government regulators and industry executives to environmental problems was to add pollution control ("tailpipe") devices to existing plants, and to build waste treatment plants. Yet, even sophisticated control equipment can only reduce—never eliminate—industrial pollutants. Confronted with this inherent shortcoming, the world is now being pushed toward more fundamental changes that can prevent pollution rather than just contain it. For example, in both Eastern and Western Europe, where heavily polluting and inefficient coal has been subsidized for decades, the push to reduce sulfur dioxide and carbon dioxide emissions is expected to cause a rapid decline in coal burning—already down by more than 20 percent in some countries. Rather than trying to add pollution control devices to outmoded power plants, industries are shifting to natural gas or investing in end-use efficiency.[12]

Improving energy efficiency is one of the most cost-effective strategies for reducing pollution. Since the seventies, considerable headway has been made, but the technical opportunities are far from exhausted. And efficiency can be improved not only in specific kinds of machinery, but in consumption patterns. In transportation, for example, switching from cars and trucks to trains will yield large savings, because trains are much more efficient.

Pollution avoidance, as distinguished from control, is catching on in many countries. Governments in Denmark, Finland, France, Germany, the Netherlands, and Norway have begun to encourage the development of "clean" technologies. In the United States, the Environmental Protection Agency (EPA) established an Office of Pollution Prevention in 1987, and ten U.S. states passed laws aimed at toxics use reduction. A growing number of companies are beginning to explore pollution prevention and waste avoidance.[13]

Manufacturing technologies can be modified to reduce waste and eliminate hazardous substances. The resulting savings often make this approach less expensive than installing pollution control equipment. In electroplating, for instance, cyanide-zinc can be replaced with alkaline noncyanide-zinc; in metal finishing, gelatin-based "subtractive" plates to reduce wastewater toxicity can substitute for lacquer-based printing press plates, and citrus-based degreasers can eliminate the need for toxic solvents. In the electronics industry, where CFCs have been used extensively to clean soldering debris from circuit boards, more benign water-based alternatives are increasingly used, and manufacturing methods are being revamped so that circuit boards do not need cleaning at all.[14]

Many products are already being replaced by more environmentally benign alternatives. For example, phosphate-free detergents and chlorine-free paper are being introduced in many countries. And synthetic chemical products are being replaced by biodegradable ones. But much greater change lies ahead. Since large amounts of energy and raw materials go into goods production (manufacturing an American car takes about as much energy as the car itself consumes in two years of driving), a move away from "planned obsolescence" is essential. And at the end of a product's useful life, recycling and reuse are preferable to the environmentally unsound practices of landfilling and incineration.[15]

Some products are indispensable in a modern society, even though current methods of their production, consumption, or disposal pose environmental problems. But there are other products whose environmental costs are out of all proportion to their utility. For them, the challenge is less to find suitable replacements than to curtail or even ban their use altogether. Much of today's packaging fits that description. In the United States, for example, as much as half of all paper production and nearly a quarter of all plastics sold go into packaging.[16]

As the economy is restructured, employment will be affected in three

> "Renewable energy employs more workers than coal or oil; recycling employs more than landfilling; and railroads more than cars."

ways. In some cases, additional jobs will be created—as in the manufacturing of pollution control devices added to existing production equipment. In other cases, employment will be substituted—as in shifting from fossil fuels to renewables, or from auto manufacturing to rail car manufacturing. In yet other circumstances, jobs may be eliminated without replacement—as, again, when packaging materials are discouraged or banned, and their production is discontinued.

Fortunately, many of the industries needed in an environmentally sustainable economy are far more labor-intensive—employ more people per dollar of output—than today's resource-based industries. Renewable energy employs more workers than coal or oil; recycling employs more than landfilling; and railroads more than cars. The employment effects will be most noticeable in extractive and basic materials industries (and in the regions, like Louisiana, Oregon, or Germany's Ruhr Valley, that depend most on them), but ultimately will cut across all sectors of the economy.

The jobs impact of a more sustainable economy will inevitably extend beyond national boundaries. To the extent that countries pursue policies that let them reduce the use of imported energy and materials, supplier nations will suffer adverse economic consequences, particularly if they depend heavily on a single commodity such as oil or bauxite. Even without the adoption of comprehensive environmental policies, developing countries are already confronted with this issue; some of the raw materials they export have been replaced by synthetic substitutes. Ecological and economic sustainability can only be addressed adequately, therefore, if the world community works cooperatively to create new industries that will both enhance the environment and provide millions of rewarding new jobs.

Pollution Abatement and Control

At first glance, the image of a more environmentally beneficent economy might be that of an industrial infrastructure elaborately equipped with advanced pollution-control equipment—a world of gleaming, smokeless smokestacks and immaculate waste-treatment plants nuzzled into pristine, parklike settings. In the next generation, the creation of millions of jobs in pollution control would seem inevitable. However, pollution control represents only the tip of the iceberg of changes to come. In the long run, far greater benefits will accrue from a fundamental restructuring of the economy to rely on industrial processes that are less polluting or destructive to begin with.

Nonetheless, pollution control is still the approach given the most attention by legislators. Some 75 to 80 percent of total pollution abatement expenditures in OECD countries are devoted to tailpipe devices, with the remainder going to preventive measures. And, pollution control will play a transitional role as industries are gradually transformed. Even if rapid progress is made toward solar and wind energy plants, or rail transit and bicycle commuting in cities, weening the world from its appetite for oil will take decades—and the need for rigorous controls will become increasingly urgent.[17]

In the past decade, pollution control expenditures—and related jobs—have increased dramatically. In 1987, the ten largest market economies spent at least $171.5 billion for pollution control. In the United States, which leads the world in pollution control expenditures by a large margin, private and public outlays (in 1989 dollars) surged from $50 billion in 1972 to $115 billion in 1989 and are expected to reach over $171 billion per year by the end of this decade. (See Figure 3.)[18]

In Asia, pollution control expenditures are expected to reach $30 billion annually by the year 2000, according to the *Journal of Commerce*. However, as some of the countries of that region confront the environmental repercussions of their rapid industrialization, their spending may push the total even higher. The South Korean Environment Ministry, for example, recently announced that it will spend nearly $11.7 billion over the next five years on a variety of clean-up programs. And Taiwan expects outlays of $35.6 billion between 1991 and 1997.[19]

In Western Europe, the pollution control market has been estimated at anywhere from $50 billion to $100 billion per year, and is projected to go as high as $150 billion annually by the end of the next decade. Germany has the largest and most developed pollution control industry in Europe, accounting for nearly 40 percent of the European Community's outlays. By contrast, the Italian and Spanish investments are much smaller than the relative size of their economies would seem to warrant.[20]

Eastern Europe and the Soviet Union will need to spend huge sums to rehabilitate their devastated environment, which could lead to a huge

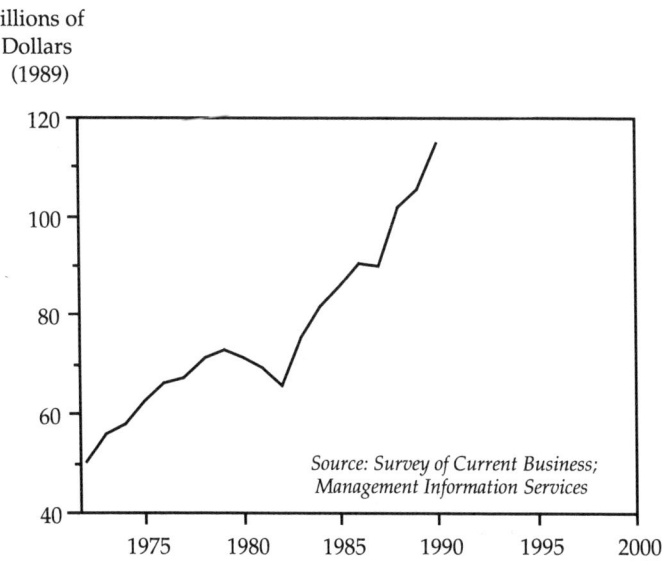

Figure 3. U.S. Pollution Abatement and Control Expenditures, 1972–90

market for pollution control equipment. But attaching expensive control devices to obsolete factories often makes little economic sense. Obsolescence instead provides an opportunity to rebuild the region's industrial capacity from scratch, using less polluting technologies. Either way, the region may rely initially on imported technology, the associated job benefits going mostly to foreign companies. Few companies in the former East Germany, for example, had relevant technological expertise. But a recent assessment by the IFO-Institut in Munich found that, given some reorientation and retraining, the existing industrial structure and skills of eastern Germany can be adapted to the needs of a pollution control industry.[21]

As the situation of the former Communist countries shows, jobs are not necessarily created where the spending originates. Instead, the employment benefits of more stringent environmental laws are likely to be reaped by those countries that develop the most sophisticated technology. And experience suggests that the nations with the best technology are those with the most stringent environmental laws. Within Western Europe, Germany and Sweden are the technological leaders, while the countries of the southern rim—Italy, Greece, Spain, and Portugal—are lagging behind. And despite their huge industrial bases, Britain and the United States also lag. Britain now imports as much environmental technology as it exports, even though as little as a decade ago its exports were eight times larger than its imports. For its desulfurization equipment, the country relies almost entirely on foreign technology. Similarly, U.S. firms buy as much as 70 percent of their air pollution-control devices from foreign manufacturers, many of them Japanese.[22]

Business executives frequently argue that new pollution control laws raise operating costs or force plant closures, impede planned investments and thus inhibit innovation, or force companies to relocate to areas with less restrictive requirements. In times of high unemployment, such arguments carry considerable weight with elected officials and the public, particularly in vulnerable communities. Like the Oregon timber companies' rhetoric pitting jobs against owls, however, these arguments find little evidence to support them.

> "Regulations can also be technology-forcing, yielding cheaper, safer, and more benign products and production processes."

Narrowly applied, the "tailpipe" approach to pollution reduction entails additional expenditures to purchase and operate control equipment that—assuming existing conditions remain unchanged—may increase production costs without raising output. However, cost estimates of complying with pollution control laws have in the past often turned out to be exaggerated—precisely because existing conditions hardly ever remain unchanged. Modifications to the production process offer substantial savings in outlays for energy and raw materials, in operating costs, and in avoided waste disposal expenses. Even where costs do increase, a company may be able to survive because price alone does not always decide whether a product can compete on the market. As a "green consumerism" takes hold, more environmentally benign products may have growing appeal, even if they are more expensive.[23]

Although they have been growing rapidly, pollution control expenditures are still relatively small. Currently, the United States and most European nations devote just 1 to 2 percent of their gross domestic product (GDP) to such programs. That share is projected to climb to 2.8 percent in the United States, and 4 percent in the Netherlands, by the year 2000. As a portion of total business investments, environmental outlays have been estimated at around 3 percent in the United States during the past two decades, as compared with 5 to 8 percent in the West German manufacturing sector. That share is much higher for the biggest polluters—the petroleum, chemicals, primary metals, and paper industries, and for mining companies and public utilities.[24]

Government regulations can impede investments and innovation by engendering or reinforcing a conservatism in product design and technology development. But regulations can also be technology-forcing, stimulating new developments that yield cheaper, safer, and more benign products and production processes. Indeed, the U.S. experience in the seventies shows that environmental rules did not slow things down. Nor, apparently, did they in Germany. In 1978, the Bundesverband der Deutschen Industrie (the national federation of industry) contended that environmental regulations were blocking 56 billion Deutsche Marks ($32 billion) worth of planned investments, and might cost jobs. But based on the BDI's own data, the IFO-Institut found that at most 5 percent of the alleged losses could legitimately be attributed to environmental regulations. In any event, the "blocked investment" scare appears to have been a red herring, as investments do not necessarily expand employment opportunities; in the mid-eighties, three quarters of all West German investments by industry were intended to increase automation—and thus reduce the number of jobs.[25]

Few jobs have been lost as a result of pollution control regulations. Studies conducted in several OECD countries have found that plants allegedly closed for environmental reasons often would have shut down anyway. The International Labour Organisation (ILO) recently concluded that environmental regulations may simply "accelerate the timing of already inevitable closing."[26]

In the United States, the EPA's Economic Dislocation Early Warning System identified 155 plant closures between 1971 and 1983, involving some 33,000 job losses, for which pollution-control laws were at least partly responsible. Painful though these losses may have been for the individuals affected, they are tiny compared to the massive layoffs taking place during that period. A McGraw-Hill survey reported that corporate executives attributed less than 1 percent of plant capacity shut down during 1976-1978 to environmental and safety regulations. The Oil, Chemical and Atomic Workers Union, meanwhile, found that of 224 plant closings between 1980 and 1986, only 5 percent occurred in response to environmental problems or regulations.[27]

Not all industries are equally affected, as the controversy over acid rain legislation demonstrates. The U.S. National Coal Association has argued that the 1990 Clean Air Act amendments could lead to the loss of 35,000 coal industry employees, or one-fifth of all jobs. However, a study prepared by ICF Resources for the EPA pegged that loss at 5,000 to 7,000 jobs by 1995 and 13,000 to 16,000 jobs by the year 2000. Any of these impacts, however, would be small compared to the actual job losses that occurred over the past decade. Stringent air quality laws clearly have the potential to cause some dislocation in coal mining, electric utilities and

> "U.S. pollution control outlays of $100 billion supported or created almost 3 million jobs."

industries like aluminum production, for which electricity is a large cost. But an analysis of acid rain bills proposed in the 99th U.S. Congress suggests that job losses would actually be more than offset by job gains.[28]

While much of the early attention of industry executives, regulators, and scholars was focused on possible negative repercussions of pollution control measures, it has become clear that the opportunities for job creation are substantial. An analysis of 1988 U.S. pollution control expenditures suggests that outlays of roughly $100 billion supported or newly created almost 3 million direct and indirect jobs. The European Community estimates that 1.2 to 1.5 million people are directly employed in pollution control activities in member countries, most of them in Germany and France. As a portion of total employment, pollution control amounts to 2.5 percent in the United States, 1.7 percent in France and the former West Germany, and approximately 1 percent for all European Community countries. As stricter pollution norms are legislated, robust growth of outlays and employment is expected in many countries.[29]

While employment gains are likely to outweigh losses resulting from environmental policies, it is not enough to compare aggregated numbers. Displaced workers may be unable to find employment in the pollution control industry if the jobs are located in different cities, regions, and industries, or require different skills. However, it appears that many of the new jobs are being created through relatively smooth adaptations. In western Germany, for example, they are typically created through the diversification of existing enterprises in the machine tool, chemical, electronics, and construction industries, rather than through the establishment of separate new companies. The skill requirements of the labor force do not appear to change much.[30]

The impacts of environmental regulations vary by region, as well as by industry. The 1990 Clean Air Act amendments provide a case in point. In order to achieve the required reductions in sulfur dioxide emissions, electric utilities are either outfitting their plants with scrubbers, making efficiency investments, or switching to natural gas or low-sulfur coal.

The job implications of these options differ widely. Ohio, Pennsylvania, Kentucky, and West Virginia, whose economies depend heavily on traditional smokestack industries, will be most directly affected. They will be cushioned against the more severe impacts, however, if pollution control predominates, because their industries may supply some of this equipment. A switch to natural gas would not be likely to cause significant regional shifts, since gas deposits are fairly widespread in much of the United States. A switch to low-sulfur coal, on the other hand, would favor mines in central Appalachia and the western United States, while high-sulfur mines in the Midwest and northern and southern Appalachia would face leaner times. Even if the volume of U.S. coal production remains unchanged, switching from eastern to western mines may reduce employment because large-scale strip mining is more prevalent, and labor productivity higher, in the West.[31]

Measured against the overall economy, pollution control programs have not had a major effect on employment. Much greater employment shifts will come with the fundamental economic restructuring of which we are now seeing just the beginning.[32]

Energy Efficiency and Renewables

Reduced consumption of fossil fuels is one of the clearest prerequisites of a sustainable energy economy. The combustion of oil and coal on a massive scale makes breathing hazardous in many cities, generates acid rain that decimates crops and forests, and is a principal contributor to global warming. Using energy more efficiently and switching from fossil fuels to renewable energy are practical ways of tackling these problems.[33]

Until recently, the belief that economic growth and high levels of employment could be achieved only with steady increases in energy use went virtually unchallenged. But after the oil crises of 1973 and 1979, experience showed that economic development and energy use could be decoupled. In fact, avoiding energy use via improved efficiency is

> "Improved efficiency is cheaper and promises more job creation than supplying energy from conventional energy sources."

cheaper and promises more job creation than supplying energy from either conventional or renewable energy sources.

On the supply side, renewables create more jobs than conventional energy industries because their capital requirements, with the exception of photovoltaic cells, are much more modest and their labor needs greater. According to a recent Worldwatch analysis, generating 1,000 gigawatt-hours of electricity per year requires 100 workers in a nuclear power plant and 116 in a coal-fired plant, but 248 in a solar thermal facility and 542 on a wind farm. German studies have reached similar conclusions.[34]

If the amount of energy required for heating, cooling, transportation, or industrial processes (not to mention the capital costs of building energy supply systems) can be reduced by relying more on conservation and renewables, then the resulting savings can be re-spent elsewhere in the economy. To the extent that such diverted spending goes to areas that are more labor-intensive than conventional energy industries, there will be a further net gain in employment. In Oregon, for instance, spending $1 million in the utility industry generates an average of 12 jobs, but the same amount spent throughout the economy yields 35 jobs.[35]

The costs and the energy and labor requirements of alternative energy technologies relative to conventional ones are bound to change. The difference in labor-intensity between fossil and solar technologies may become less pronounced, as equipment for the latter is manufactured in larger batches and the new facilities become more automated. Another important factor is the cost of conventional energy. Oil prices have been on a rollercoaster for the past two decades, and they are now much lower than in the late seventies and early eighties. But there is growing recognition that the market price for oil does not reflect the enormous environmental damage inflicted by its use, and many countries have recently raised energy taxes at least partly to incorporate these non-monetary costs into conventional cost-accounting. As energy prices are pushed upward, rising investment in efficiency and alternative energy sources is likely to create a host of new jobs.

Residential weatherization—including such measures as caulking and weather-stripping, ceiling and floor insulation, installation of storm windows and doors, and duct insulation—is a particularly labor-intensive process. A study by Steve Colt of the University of Alaska at Anchorage found that state spending on weatherization creates more jobs per dollar of outlays than any other type of capital project—almost three times as many direct jobs as highway construction, for example. Some $42 million spent on Alaska's low-income weatherization program from 1978 through 1989 yielded a total of 752 job-years of employment, including 380 job-years of direct (weatherization) jobs, 194 indirect (working for suppliers), and 178 induced (working for businesses in which the weatherization workers' income was spent).[36]

In the United States, the highest expenditures on low-income weatherization are in New York. The Center for the Biology of Natural Systems (CBNS) at Queens College, New York City, analyzed the economic impact of the state's Weatherization Assistance Program from 1976 to 1989, and found that as of 1989, a total of 254,000 housing units, or 14 percent of those eligible, had been weatherized at a cost of $368 million (in 1985 dollars). The CBNS study estimated that roughly 23,000 to 30,000 job-years of net employment was generated during that period, or 60 to 80 jobs per $1 million of expenditure.[37]

Across the United States, 4.2 million low-income households, or 19 percent of those eligible, have so far been weatherized at a cost of $4.5 billion. Although New York state is not entirely representative of conditions nationwide, the CBNS findings permit a rough approximation of the number of jobs that could be created if all low-income housing units were weatherized. Keeping in mind that average U.S. weatherization costs per unit are 30 percent lower than in New York, a total of 1.4 to 1.8 million job-years might be generated. Assuming that similar conditions hold for weatherizing all U.S. households, the total weatherization job potential is 6 to 7 million job-years.[38]

Incorporating energy efficiency into new building designs allows greater energy savings and, thus, indirectly generates more jobs than

> "If all U.S. low-income housing units were weatherized, a total of 1.4 to 1.8 million job-years might be generated."

retrofitting does. For example, an Idaho study by Economic Research Associates found that the implementation of a building code requiring greater energy efficiency than current state standards would reduce residential use of electricity 46 percent. The energy savings exceeded the additional construction costs, and one new job was created for every 1.5 million kilowatt-hours conserved.[39]

One of the most comprehensive studies of the economic impact of a substantial commitment to solar and conservation in the United States was prepared in 1979 by Leonard Rodberg for the Joint Economic Committee of the U.S. Congress. Assuming an annual investment of $115 billion (in 1989 dollars), Rodberg found that more than two million jobs might have been created in 10 years—a quarter of them in conservation and the rest in solar energy. The decrease in consumption of non-renewable fuels—45 quadrillion BTUs (quads) less by 1990 than was projected at the time under a business-as-usual approach—would have led to the loss of about one million jobs in primary-energy and electricity-generating industries. But re-spending the associated savings in energy outlays elsewhere in the economy would have brought additional employment gains, for a net increase of almost three million jobs in the economy as a whole.[40]

More recently, a study was prepared for the Great Lakes Governors to determine the economic effects of increasing the use of biomass energy. In 1985, over 32,000 people in the Great Lakes states were employed in jobs directly or indirectly associated with this energy source. Increasing the use of biomass by 50 percent between 1985 and 1995 would generate 50,900 new jobs in operations and maintenance, 17,500 in manufacturing and construction of new plants and equipment, and 7,900 through the re-spending of savings. Taking into account the jobs lost by displacement of fossil fuels, the net gain is still 42,100 by 1995. The bulk of the employment gains would be in agriculture, fabricated metal products, and wholesale and retail trade.[41]

A study prepared in 1985 for the Commission of the European Community (EC) analyzed the employment potential of six energy conservation and renewable energy technologies in Britain, Denmark, France, and West Germany. It found that some 34 million tons of oil equivalent (mtoe) could be saved and an average of 142,000 job-years gained by the year 2000. Since only six technologies and four out of 12 member countries were included in the study, the authors suggest that a full-fledged conservation and renewables program could yield, for the EC as a whole, a minimum of 530,000 job-years, or an average of about 3,800 jobs per mtoe of primary energy saved.[42]

While a shift from fossil fuels to solar energy entails job losses in the former, there are overlaps among the kinds of suppliers and skills required. For example, materials needed for the production of solar collectors for space and water heating include glass or plastic for the collector cover, copper, aluminum, and steel for frames and absorber plates, and fiberglass or a rigid foam for insulation. The prospective suppliers are all established industries. The U.S. Geological Survey estimated in the seventies that solar heating and cooling systems capable of replacing 0.6 quads of conventional fuel consumption per year would require over 5 million tons of aluminum, over 7 million tons of glass, and close to 10 million tons of iron.[43]

Many of the skills needed for manufacturing solar systems are "similar to those required for conventional construction projects and heating system installation," according to Rodberg. Thus, work opportunities exist for a variety of occupations, including sheet metal workers, carpenters, plumbers, pipefitters, and construction workers.[44]

The economies that would gain the most by boosting efficiency and substituting locally available renewables are those that now depend on imported energy. The losers would be those regions and countries whose economies depend on the export of fossil fuels—mainly in the Middle East. Such countries will need support to broaden their economic base as the world checks its thirst for fossil fuels.[45]

To date, the solar and conservation potential remains largely unfulfilled, though millions of people in developing countries are now employed

> "While a shift from fossil fuels to solar energy entails job losses in the former, there are overlaps among the kinds of suppliers and skills required."

processing charcoal and other biomass fuels. Unfortunately, low oil prices and a lack of tax incentives and government research and development support have held back the commercial take-off of many of the renewable industries. U.S. solar employment, for example, was estimated at only about 20,000 in the mid-eighties. Nonetheless, many of the renewable energy sources are now poised for rapid growth, propelled by new government policies that take account of their environmental advantages compared to fossil fuels.

Already, solar photovoltaic cells are being installed in rural homes throughout the developing world, and worldwide output increased 16-fold between 1980 and 1990. Solar thermal power stations are providing 350 megawatts of electricity in southern California. And in other parts of that state some 15,000 wind machines are generating enough power to meet all the residential needs of San Francisco. It will not be long before these and other renewable energy industries provide large numbers of jobs.[46]

Railroads versus Highways

Transportation is a major user of fossil fuels, and therefore an important source of urban air pollution, acid rain, and global warming. The assumption of indefinite access to cheap, abundant energy supplies has, particularly in North America and Australia, led to the growth of sprawling residential settlements that make car ownership indispensable. Yet, what is essential today will be untenable tomorrow. By avoiding unnecessary sprawl, future urban designs may facilitate such activities as commuting and shopping with less dependence on motor vehicles and greater reliance on walking and biking. This naturally will have a big impact on jobs.[47]

Just as suburbanization has spawned long, gas-guzzling commutes for millions of workers, the modern industrial production system is characterized by reliance on long supply lines for raw materials and other inputs. On the marketing end, consumer goods are often shipped thousands of kilometers even when they are locally available in sufficient quantity and quality. "Sending coals to Newcastle," once considered a foolish absurdity, has become a routine practice in modern commerce.

Many nations are awakening to their unhealthy addiction to a mode of transportation that is excessively energy-intensive and polluting. While recent attempts to mitigate these problems have focused on limited measures such as catalytic converters, alternative fuels and, to a lesser extent, improved fuel economy, the magnitude of the challenge suggests that a wholesale restructuring of the transportation industry is required to make it sustainable. At present, a shift from cars and trucks toward railroads, subways, light rail lines, and buses offers alternative job opportunities for at least part of the workforce that now manufactures, assembles, operates, or services cars and trucks. In the decades to come, however, a more radical reorientation aimed at reducing overall transportation needs, and increasing the share of non-motorized modes, may ultimately mean fewer jobs in transportation.[48]

The motor vehicle industry is a cornerstone of the modern industrial economy. It contributes almost 7 percent of global economic output and employs more than 4 million workers. Automobiles account for about 4 percent of all industrial employment in the United States and Spain, 6 percent in Britain and Canada, 7 percent in Japan, and 8 to 9 percent in France, Italy, Sweden, and the former West Germany. Vehicle sales continue to grow, but due to automation, employment has expanded much less. For example, sales revenues for West German auto companies more than doubled from 1977 to 1987, but the number of jobs grew by less than one quarter.[49]

Rail systems virtually everywhere have been systematically disadvantaged. For example, Deutsche Bundesbahn, the German federal railway system, has steadily lost ground in both passenger and freight transport. Between 1967 and the late eighties, its share fell from 9 to 6 percent of passenger transportation and from 31 to 22 percent of freight transport. Moreover, the railway's investment in a few high-speed passenger train connections comes increasingly at the expense of maintaining service on lesser routes. In freight transport, the railway system seems destined to

> "In the decades to come, reducing overall transportation needs, and increasing the share of non-motorized modes, may ultimately mean fewer jobs in transportation."

become a mere adjunct to trucking. All told, employment has been cut in half in the postwar period, to the point where schedules often cannot be met and the remaining employees are forced to work overtime. In the former East Germany, similar problems loom as cars and trucks take center stage in the wake of unification with the West. A quarter of the 250,000-strong rail workforce is to be laid off over the next five years.[50]

While the railroads languish, the trucking industry is booming. In western Germany, it has grown almost five-fold between 1960 and 1988, capturing 56 percent of the country's freight transport. Employment grew almost 50 percent between 1978 and 1989. The trucking boom in Europe is likely to continue for some years, fueled by lowered tariff barriers in the European Community, the opening of commerce with Eastern Europe, and growing adoption of the "just-in-time" system of production, whereby factories rely on frequent, precisely timed deliveries of materials and parts.[51]

Considering the priority accorded cars and trucks, it is not surprising that these industries provide more jobs than does public transportation. Indeed, highway vehicle-related jobs in the former West Germany outnumber rail-related jobs by 5 to 1. (See Table 3.) Since the data omit jobs both at supplier firms for rail-vehicle manufacturing and in track construction and maintenance, however, that ratio is actually overstated and may be closer to 3 to 1. This imbalance is much more severe in the United States, where car reliance is higher, inter-city rail transport is mostly limited to freight, and the manufacture of trolleys and subway cars has virtually ceased. And due to rising automation, U.S. freight railroad employment has been cut almost in half during the past decade.[52]

An environmentally sustainable economy will require a reversal of the still-rising dependence on cars and trucks. For this to happen, rail-based transport will need to be given priority. In some respects, the transportation system of the future will resemble that of 80 or 100 years ago, before the automotive revolution. It will not be a true return to the past, howev-

Table 3. Land Transportation Employment, West Germany, 1987–89

Activity	Jobs (Thousands)	Share[1] (Percent)
Motor Vehicles	2,507	83
Manufacturing & Repair of Motor Vehicles[2]	1,680	55
Automotive Dealers	300	10
Gasoline Stations and Other Services	100	3
Truck Freight Transport	427	14
Rail	523	17
Railway and Light Rail Manufacturing	100	3
Railways	277	9
Urban Mass Transit Systems	146	5
Grand Total	**3,030**	**100**

[1]Totals may not add due to rounding. [2]Including supplier firms.

Sources: Compiled from Markus Hesse and Rainer Lucas, *Verkehrswende. Ökologische und Soziale Orientierungen für die Verkehrswirtschaft*, Schriftenreihe des IÖW 39/90 (Berlin and Wuppertal: Institut für Ökologische Wirtschaftsforschung, 1990); Markus Hesse and Rainer Lucas, *Die Beschäftigungspolitische Bedeutung der Verkehrswirtschaft in Nordrhein-Westfalen*, Forschungsprojekt im Auftrag des Instituts für Landes- und Stadtentwicklungsforschung (Berlin and Wuppertal: IÖW, 1990).

er, since there are now great opportunities for technological and other improvements. Many new jobs will be created in public transport, and they will be less exposed to the vagaries of world market pressures than most auto-related jobs.[53]

Although the car and trucking industries employ millions of people, their contribution to the overall job market is not commensurate with their dollar output. German figures show that highway construction generates the fewest jobs of any public infrastructure investment. Spending 1 billion Deutsche Marks ($580 million) on highways yields only 14,000 to 19,000 jobs, as compared with about 22,000 jobs in railway tracks, or 23,000 in light rail track construction. Similarly, a 1988 assessment found that the number of jobs created in building urban bike paths compares favorably with that in highway construction.[54]

One of the most important employment questions is the extent to which the skills now used in the automotive industries are adaptable to the operation of rail systems. Marcus Hesse and Rainer Lucas of the Institute for Ecological Economics Research in Wuppertal, Germany, conclude that given some overlaps and similarities in skill patterns, the shifts should not be too difficult. Both motor vehicle manufacturing and railroads require a broad distribution of occupations. The skills (engineering, concrete pouring, trucking, etc.) needed to construct highways, railway tracks, and bike paths are relatively similar, although workers will need to adapt from one to another.[55]

With proper preparation, the disruptions caused by shifting to public transportation can be kept to a minimum. However, more jobs may be lost if societies move to redesign cities to bring employment and commercial centers closer to residential centers, thereby reducing the need for transportation. But the latter goal will take longer to achieve, allowing for a relatively smooth transition.

Recycling Materials, Retaining Jobs

From extraction to processing and disposal, the use of raw materials—wood, metals, and minerals—requires large amounts of water and energy, and inflicts immense damage on the environment. However, most products can be made to incorporate fewer materials while providing the same services. And instead of designing goods for quick disposal, making them more sturdy allows for their repair and reuse. In short, avoidance is the best strategy for reducing the volume of trash that releases heavy metals, dioxins, furans, and other pollutants into the environment. At the end of a product's useful life, recycling offers the best means of reducing the waste stream and energy needed to manufacture products from virgin materials.[56]

Recycling is already an important source of jobs (it may actually be as important an employer as coal mining in the United States), but no government statistics on recycling jobs are compiled and comparatively little research has been done on the subject. Jim Quigley of the CBNS has surveyed various recycling operations to determine how much material it takes, per year, to create one job. Assessing programs in several U.S. states, he found that recycling programs vary widely in their labor intensity, but generate on average one job for every 465 tons of materials handled each year. Put differently, for each million tons of waste, approximately 2,000 jobs are created. Using that figure, Quigley calculates that under current conditions—with roughly 10 percent of the 200 million tons of municipal solid waste generated in the United States each year being recycled—more than 43,000 people may be employed. Other studies suggest that the number is even higher. The ALCOA company estimates that at least 30,000 people in the United States are involved in the recycling of aluminum alone—equal to twice the employment in the primary aluminum production industry. And boosting the recycling rate would open up a far larger number of jobs. According to Quigley, increasing the rate to 75 percent could yield some 375,000 jobs in the United States.[57]

Compared with incineration and landfilling, recycling offers more employment and is still the cheaper alternative, due to its much lower capital requirements. The construction of waste-burning plants and the manufacturing of the machinery they use create more temporary jobs than the more modestly equipped recycling centers do, but recycling offers a large number of permanent jobs in operations and maintenance activities. For each one million tons of materials processed, recycling facilities in Vermont, for example, generate about 550 to 2,000 jobs, depending on the kind and size of facility. But for incinerators, the range is 150 to 1,100 and for landfills it is 50 to 360 jobs. Facilities in New York City are much larger, and the resulting economies of scale mean that more waste is handled per employee than in Vermont. The key results, however, are the same: recycling creates more jobs than do either landfills or incinerators. (See Figure 4.)[58]

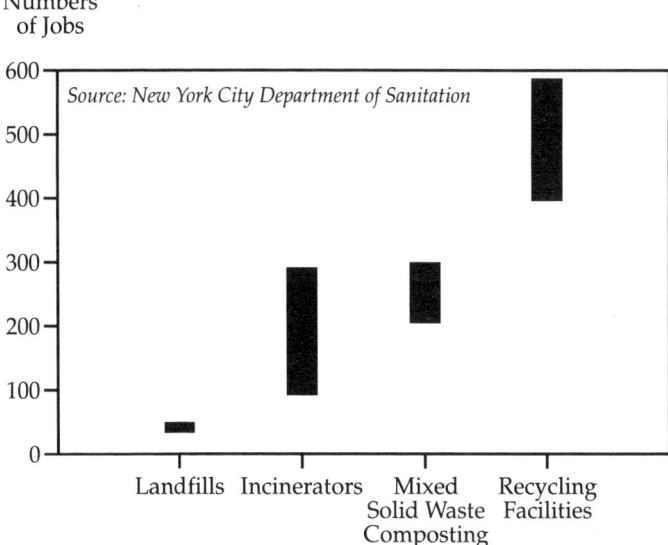

Figure 4. Jobs per 1 Million Tons of Waste Processed, New York City (Range for Facilities of Different Capacities)

According to Barry Commoner, director of CBNS, an improved materials recovery program could boost the recycling rate in New York City from 18 percent to 75 percent. Pursuing that route instead of burning waste would both save money and create new jobs. At about $500 million, the cost of building an incinerator is three times that of recycling facilities that can handle the same amount of trash. Even a more modest goal—recycling one quarter of the city's waste by April 1994 as mandated by law—would create about 1,400 jobs, or more than four times the number generated if the same volume of waste were incinerated.[59]

While recycling offers large economic benefits, the gain is not without pain. Recycling implies, after all, that fewer raw materials are mined, smelted, and made into products. Recycling aluminum beverage cans, for example, means that less bauxite is needed, with inevitable repercussions in producer countries such as Australia, Jamaica, and Guinea. And there will be fewer jobs in the energy industry, since aluminum recycling saves energy compared to aluminum produced from virgin materials. The same is true for glass recycling, and even more so for glass re-use (re-using a bottle instead of melting it to make new glass). Recycling paper inevitably means less demand for wood pulp, and fewer jobs in logging and paper mills.

Still, these losses may not be large, since the energy and wood pulp industries are not big employers. Quigley, for example, has calculated that the 3 million tons of waste newspaper recycled in the United States in 1987 (one quarter of the total annual newsprint consumption) may have displaced up to 7,400 jobs. The overall job gains are still likely to outweigh the losses, however. A 1986 West German study, for example, showed that although increasing the share of throw-away beverage containers from 15 percent to 90 percent would create an additional 15,000 to 20,000 jobs, the implied abandonment of reusable and recyclable bottles would at the same time cause the loss of 90,000 jobs. Thus, the fledgling recycling industry has already become an important employer—and offers the potential for many more jobs in the future.[60]

Sustainable Forestry: From Logging to Stewardship

In our urban society, the misconstrued conflict between environmental and economic well-being is often fought most bitterly over some of the resources least seen or understood: the old-growth forests. With their ancient trees—many dating back hundreds of years, and a few reaching back thousands—these forests have acquired a mystique that stimulates imaginations and arouses passions among conservationists. Considered major sanctuaries of biodiversity, they have become battlegrounds in a struggle over basic human priorities—as focused in the "owls versus jobs" debate. The passion of environmentalists is fully matched by the ire of loggers, who—often rightly—see their livelihoods as threatened.

> "The old-growth forests have become battlegrounds in a struggle over basic human priorities—as focused in the 'owls versus jobs' debate."

In the U.S. Pacific Northwest, the preservation of the remaining old-growth stands—habitat critical to the survival of the northern spotted owl—has become a top objective for environmentalists. A lawsuit was filed in 1987 to protect the threatened bird from extinction, setting off an acrimonious dispute. In April, 1990, a task force of government scientists issued the so-called "Thomas Report," which determined that the spotted owl was an endangered species and recommended that over 3 million acres of federal forest land be set aside as protected habitat. A year later, the Fish and Wildlife Service proposed logging restrictions for 11.6 million acres of forest in Washington, Oregon, and California. And in a May, 1991 ruling, a federal judge suspended timber sales in 66,000 acres of federal forests and ordered the Forest Service to draft a protection plan for the spotted owl by March, 1992.[61]

The spotted owl issue epitomizes some of the distortions that have characterized the jobs-versus-environment debate. On one hand, the focus on a single endangered species, intrinsically important as it is, has drawn much of the public's attention away from the larger challenge of protecting complex ecosystems that play vital roles in maintaining the health of thousands of other species as well—including our own. Likewise, it overlooks the other benefits of old growth forests, such as their roles in the purification of water, cleansing of air, prevention of soil erosion, and stabilization of climate—not to mention providing opportunities for human recreation. On the other hand, the focus on lost logging jobs has overlooked the larger impacts on employment.

Timber industry officials assert that as many as 150,000 jobs could be lost if the Thomas plan is implemented, though the task force itself estimated the number at 12,000 to 20,000. The Forest Service and the Bureau of Land Management (BLM), meanwhile, claim that saving the spotted owl would cost up to 28,000 jobs by the year 2000, including indirect and induced employment. None of these studies, however, take into consideration future job losses that, due to mechanization, would occur even in the absence of any environmental measures. In addition, they fail to account for positive employment effects of old-growth forest protection.[62]

The Pacific Northwest timber industry was shedding jobs well before the spotted owl controversy erupted. And future employment prospects are clouded not so much because of environmental restrictions but for three other reasons: the industry is literally running out of its own resource; it continues to mechanize its operations; and it exports large quantities of unprocessed logs.

No more than 10 to 15 percent of an estimated 15 to 19 million acres of original old-growth forest in the Pacific Northwest remain today. Darius Adams of the University of Washington expects timber harvests on public land in the western United States to drop by at least 40 percent by the year 2000, even without environment-inspired limits. The strong emphasis on short-term profit maximization during the eighties has accelerated the cutting process in some cases. So-called "leveraged buyouts" that liquidate a company's assets to finance its own takeover have led timber companies to engage in massive clear-cutting operations that rapidly exhaust the forest resource base and imperil long-term employment. In the Pacific Northwest, conservationists estimate that at current cutting rates all old-growth logging will disappear within 20 years.[63]

From 1977 to 1987, logging in Oregon's national forests increased by 16 percent, but timber employment dropped—due to automation—by more than 12,000 jobs, or 15 percent. It took 10 workers to process one million board feet of wood in 1977, compared to 8 workers ten years later. Those workers who retained their jobs were forced to take pay cuts of up to 25 percent in order to compete with non-union loggers in the southeastern United States. And, future job losses from automation are likely to far exceed any losses that might result from environmental protection measures. Jeff DeBonis, founder of the Association of Forest Service Employees for Environmental Ethics, argues that "even if the current, unsustainable level of cut continued for the next 45 years, the Pacific Northwest wood products industry would still lose at least 35,000 jobs" due to mechanization.[64]

Timber companies often find it profitable to export unprocessed logs. In 1988, one quarter of the cut in Oregon and Washington was exported in

> "Future job losses from automation are likely to far exceed any losses that might result from environmental protection measures."

the form of raw logs. Jeff Olson, an economist with the Wilderness Society in Portland, has calculated that the United States loses 4 to 5 jobs for every one million board feet of unprocessed logs exported. A recent Forest Service/BLM report whose publication the Bush administration sought to suppress suggests that a ban on shipping raw logs abroad would generate some 15,000 domestic jobs. Other proponents of such a policy have presented even higher estimates.[65]

If current trends continue, the job outlook for the timber industry will be bleak with or without environmental policies. Yet there is a silver lining: the economy of the Pacific Northwest region is becoming more broadly-based and less dependent on timber extraction. Between 1975 and 1987, all other sectors of the economy in that region grew rapidly. As a result, the logging and wood products industry's share of the gross product of Washington and Oregon dropped by half, to 3.5 percent.[66]

Timber-dependent areas in other countries face comparable problems. In the province of British Columbia, Canada, for example, timber jobs declined by 25 percent during the eighties—the result of overcutting, automation, and a market slump. But the British Columbian timber industry is more pivotal to the regional economy than is its U.S. counterpart. It accounts for 15 percent of all Provincial employment if indirect and induced jobs are included. Still, the Canadian Forest Resources Commission calculates that a hypothetical 10 percent reduction in wood supply would cause only a 2 percent job loss. And that finding does not take into account the economic benefits arising from forest uses other than logging. In areas like British Columbia and the Australian island of Tasmania, timber is a much larger part of the economy than in the U.S. Pacific Northwest, so major changes in logging industry practices in those regions would be considerably harder for their respective economies to absorb.[67]

Unless displaced loggers and mill workers receive assistance to make the transition to new careers, the availability of jobs in other industries will be of little comfort. While the Pacific Northwest economy as a whole is becoming more diversified, individual communities may have few immediate alternatives. The U.S. Forest Service could alleviate the problem by providing temporary income support for loggers instead of subsidizing logging on federal lands, but the Bush administration opposes any special aid program.

The Redwood Employee Protection program, set up for workers displaced by the expansion of the Redwood National Park in the late seventies, provided salaries, fringe benefits, pensions, and training and relocation benefits. Its record is mixed, since it failed to bring new jobs to the lumber towns or to initiate any innovative training programs. Richard Kazis and Richard Grossman have commented in their book *Fear at Work*, that "a large number of former lumber-jacks and millworkers have been left to grow hopeless on the government dole." And even though the timber companies had reaped sizeable profits, they were not required to contribute anything to the program.[68]

Despite the animosity between loggers and environmentalists, efforts are underway to bridge the gulf of misunderstanding and develop a joint approach. Headwaters, an environmental group based in southern Oregon, hopes to help communities overcome their dependence on extractive resources and adapt to the demands of a sustainable economy. Together with other organizations, it has been working with local union woodworkers to set up two worker-owned companies to seek forest management contracts and to process, ship, and market forest products. They plan to use natural selection methods that allow the harvest of other products besides timber. Another example is the Labor-Environmental Assessment and Planning Project (LEAPP) in Oregon. Still in its formative stage, LEAPP intends to study the implications and feasibility of extensive environmental reclamation and restoration activities.[69]

The aim of the so-called new forestry is to reshape logging practices to maintain biodiversity; reduce or eliminate spraying, fertilizing, or burning; retain sufficiently large reserved lands; protect riparian zones; and reduce the use of roads and machines. Overall, the aim is to reduce the volume of timber harvested in heavily-cut areas. Ideally, the logger would be transformed into a steward of the forest, with intimate knowledge about the complexity of the ecosystem. Cutting trees would be supplanted by other activities such as harvesting fruits, fodder, and medicinal plants. (For example, the bark of the Pacific yew tree is a source of taxol, which can be used to produce an anti-cancer drug). Reforestation activities and small-scale logging operations tend to be highly labor-intensive. Making the transition from a purely extractive industry to stewardship requires considerable training and education—and will open up professional opportunities in such areas as silviculture, botany, marketing, planning, and communication.[70]

Severe degradation now afflicts large areas of the world's forests, and massive restoration efforts are needed if the goal of a sustainable forestry is to be achieved. Such efforts can also provide much work in replanting clear-cut areas, digging up and reseeding logging roads, and restoring streams. While these tasks may not necessarily present profit-making opportunities for timber companies, they are essential for the survival not just of endangered species like the northern spotted owl, but for the earth as a whole.

Making the Transition

As the world moves toward an economy that emphasizes reduction in the absolute amounts of materials processed, as well as substitutions in the kinds of materials consumed, profound changes in the job market are inevitable. Any major industrial shift is likely to be painful, and as this one proceeds, there is much for policymakers to be concerned about. The extractive and basic materials industries, in particular, are bound to be hit hard. Whole classes of workers and age groups may find their jobs threatened. Some regions may see their industrial base disappear. And lack of education or training may leave many workers ill equipped to find jobs in a sustainable economy.

A well-planned, forward-looking government policy is thus essential if societies are to ensure that their citizens have rewarding jobs in the future. No longer can they afford to simply leave the jobs question to the "free market," or to maintain the disincentives to job creation that are embodied in many existing policies. New policies are needed to encourage the development of non-polluting manufacturing and processing technologies, to stimulate the production of more benign and durable goods, and to establish markets for them.

Today, private investment decisions are distorted by massive subsidies that favor the exploitation of virgin materials, the consumption of nonrenewable sources of energy, and reliance on highly polluting modes of transportation. To foster greater energy efficiency, the reuse and recycling of materials, and the development of renewable energy sources and public transportation systems, these subsidies need to be phased out. With the help of tax incentives, redirected public infrastructure programs, and a well-formulated public research and development program, the groundwork for a sustainable future can be laid. Regionally-targeted incentives can attract new investment to those areas most affected by the decline or disappearance of heavily polluting industries. Where market forces alone are insufficient, government procurement programs can stir demand for environmentally sound products.

The development of more sustainable industrial policies can also be facilitated by improved public access to information about the environmental impacts of specific corporate activities. Employers faced with environmental regulations may be tempted to use the threat of job layoffs as a cudgel to thwart needed legislation. In the United States, some public "right-to-know" legislation exists, but its scope is limited. The Clean Air Act and Clean Water Act include provisions that give workers who have been laid off because of their employers' compliance with these laws the right to request an EPA investigation—but only after the closure of a factory has taken place. The establishment of corporate "eco-audits" (detailing environmental impacts of products, production processes, and materials handled) would allow workers and communities to confront environmental job blackmail—and make it clear to employees and the public alike that economic and environmental health are interdependent.[71]

> "Corporate 'eco-audits' would allow workers and communities to confront environmental job blackmail."

Although a sustainable economy promises to create a host of new jobs, the transition is likely to be difficult for some industries, regions, and communities. That difficulty will be compounded by the high levels of unemployment that already exist. Automation continues to make many positions obsolete even as millions of young people search for work each year. A variety of measures—restructuring corporate taxes, providing retraining assistance and income support to displaced workers, and sharing work more equitably—could help to provide more job opportunities, and to smooth the transition process.

Increasing labor productivity is almost universally regarded as an indication of economic progress, but this easy assumption may no longer hold true. There is nothing inherent in technological innovation that dictates an unending march toward using more capital and fewer workers. Products and production technologies can be designed to employ larger numbers of people, reducing unemployment without sacrificing industrial productivity.

Unfortunately, the existing economy compels many corporate managers to seek competitive advantage by eliminating jobs. The move to a sustainable economy demands recognition of a new interpretation of "progress"—one that is better able to tap human creativity rather than stifle it. Although wages and salaries account for a large share of the economy's total costs, replacing workers with machines can have unintended effects: the loss of experience, ingenuity, and dexterity that are unique to human beings and crucial to producing high-quality goods.[72]

A restructuring of the tax system could help to make employing more people, rather than more machines, appealing to companies. One proposal envisions a levy on corporate energy use as a financing mechanism for social security funds. The levy would permit a reduction in the social security tax rate, perhaps by as much as one third. For employers, gross wage costs would decline even though net wages remain unaffected. Labor would become relatively less costly, and therefore more attractive to employers. While labor-saving machinery already installed would not be abandoned, the proposal would help put a brake on future job displacements. A West German proposal estimated that, depending on the size of an energy levy and the degree to which employers rely on overtime, the demand for labor could grow by 750,000 to 1.5 million jobs, or 3 to 6 percent of the country's total employment in 1988.[73]

A more direct way to encourage job creation (or at least to discourage further job elimination) is to tie corporate tax rates to an employment-based formula, such as the number of jobs per dollar of sales revenue. To be workable, the tax would not be based on comparative labor-intensities among different industries, but on the amount of progress made within each industry. Because the energy tax and a job-linked tax have a dual objective—generating revenues and achieving structural changes in the economy—they suffer from a built-in dilemma: to the extent that they accomplish the desired restructuring, the revenue base shrinks. They will therefore need to be gradually readjusted over time.[74]

Another financial instrument in need of recalibration is the capital depreciation allowance. Setting depreciation schedules is a difficult task because different kinds of production equipment wear out at different rates. But to the extent that companies are permitted to write off taxes on machinery at a rate faster than actual wear-out occurs, the cost of capital is effectively lowered and the replacement of workers by machines encouraged.[75]

No matter how many jobs will eventually be created in a sustainable society, there is still a need to provide assistance to workers who lose their jobs due to the decline of polluting industries. Existing laws provide some training, income support, counseling and placement services, and relocation assistance, but are clearly not equal to the task. U.S. federal outlays for worker retraining have been slashed by 50 percent since 1980. In 1987, public spending on employment and training programs, measured as a share of GDP, came to only 0.3 percent in the United States, compared with 0.7 percent in Britain, France, and Spain, 1 percent in West Germany, and 1.7 percent in Sweden.[76]

In the United States, the Oil, Chemical and Atomic Workers Union has

> "U.S. federal outlays for worker retraining have been slashed by 50 percent since 1980."

proposed the creation of a comprehensive "Superfund for Workers" to provide those workers displaced from environmentally destructive industries with up to four years of financial support to allow them to pursue vocational retraining or a career shift through an extended program of study. The proposal envisions full tuition and income support including fringe benefits. Possible variations include seed money and other assistance to help start a small business, or partial income supplements for those who seek less well-paid work. The annual cost for one million workers might come to $40 billion. Not all of this would be a net addition to public expenditures, however, because funds currently devoted to unemployment compensation and other assistance programs could be marshaled for this purpose—and because a program that enables laid-off workers to become active participants in the economy again also adds to tax revenues.[77]

During the 1990 Clean Air Act amendments debate, Sen. Robert Byrd and Rep. Robert Wise, both of West Virginia, proposed "termination benefits" for coal miners who lose their jobs as a direct result of acid rain provisions in the Act reauthorization. Similarly, Senators Bob Packwood (Oregon) and Slade Gorton (Washington) introduced legislation that would use a portion of the proceeds from federal timber sales to aid communities and workers hurt by logging cutbacks. The next step is to link such programs to the tax, investment, and research and development policies needed to bring about the shift toward sustainability. However, neither these legislative forays nor the Worker Superfund proposal are designed to complement this far reaching restructuring of the economy.[78]

Considering that large numbers of people are already out of work, and more are seeking work for the first time every year, the challenge is not only to create as many rewarding jobs as possible, but to share available work more equitably. European trade unions have long championed worktime reductions as a means of providing employment for more people. Reducing the length of time that individual employees spend at the workplace could be accomplished by shortening hours, cutting the number of work days per week, extending vacation time, lowering the retirement age, offering parental leave and sabbaticals for continued education, or experimenting with job-sharing arrangements. Individual countries vary widely in the length of average annual worktime and therefore their potential for reductions. (See Table 4.)[79]

Although many people prefer to spend less time in the factory or at the office, working fewer hours often is not a practical option for them, because in a commodity-intensive economy they are compelled to seek full-time employment. Yet, a key component of sustainability, the production of more durable goods, provides a crucial underpinning for such a move. When goods do not wear out rapidly, they need not be replaced as frequently. More durable goods are likely to be more expensive than throw-aways; but over time, people will spend less money on purchases of furniture, appliances, and clothing. Hence there is less need for paid work to achieve a given material standard of living.[80]

Table 4. Average Weekly Hours Worked per Employee in Manufacturing, Selected Countries, 1950-89[1]

Country	1950	1980	1989	Decline 1950–89
				(Percent)
Sweden	41	28	30	28
West Germany	44	33	31	30
France	38	33	31	18
Britain	41	35	36	13
Italy	38	34	36	6
United States	38	36	38	1
Japan	44	42	41	6

[1]All numbers are rounded.

Source: Worldwatch Institute, calculated from U.S. Department of Labor, Bureau of Labor Statistics, Office of Productivity and Technology, "Underlying Data for Indexes of Output per Hour, HourlyCompensation, and Unit Labor Costs in Manufacturing, Twelve Industrial Countries, 1950-1989, and Unit Labor Costs in Korea and Taiwan, 1970-1989," Washington, D.C., May 1991.

A more sustainable economy promises great environmental and economic benefits, though the transition will not be without pain. It will produce many losers, particularly among extractive and heavy industries. But the evidence is strong that the winners will outnumber the losers: more jobs will be created in energy efficiency, recycling, and public transportation than will be lost in the oil and coal industries, car manufacturing, and waste disposal. In fact, automation is a much more important cause of job loss than environmental protection is. And while extractive industries tend to be geographically concentrated, jobs arising out of energy conservation, renewables, and recycling are likely to be more evenly spread.

Most new jobs will not require radically new skills. To build and operate a wind power plant, for example, requires the services of a variety of familiar, well-established trades and occupations. Meteorologists and surveyors are needed to select and rate appropriate sites; structural engineers to design the wind turbines and supervise their assembly; metal workers to supply the rotors; mechanics and computer operators to monitor the system and keep it in good working order. New ways of extracting and using energy, new kinds of products, and a new quality of life will still depend on long-established human capabilities and skills.

The overall trends—for industry and for the world—will be profound, but for individual workers the stress of change will be no more than it has been for the past century. As happened with the automobile revolution and the advent of computerization, some individuals will struggle with dislocation and the need to learn new job skills, while many more will find new opportunities.

Shifting to an environmentally sustainable society is a task equal in its scope, complexity, and ultimate importance to the profound transformations wrought by the Industrial Revolution. What is different now is that humanity already has at its disposal many of the tools and much of the knowledge required to make the transition. It still needs to gather the vision and political will to embrace the policies that can save the planet.

Notes

1. Organisation for Economic Co-operation and Development (OECD), *Historical Statistics 1960-1988* (Paris, December 1990).

2. One of the major controversies of the sustainability theme concerns the question of economic growth. Daly and Cobb, Jr. distinguish between "growth" as "quantitative expansion in the scale of the physical dimensions of the economic system" and "development" as "qualitative change of a physically nongrowing economic system in dynamic equilibrium with the environment." "Sustainable development" is thus a possibility and necessity while "sustainable growth" is self-contradictory. Herman E. Daly and John B. Cobb, Jr., *For the Common Good. Redirecting the Economy Toward Community, the Environment, and a Sustainable Future* (Boston: Beacon Press, 1989).

3. Lucinda Wykle et al., *Worker Empowerment in a Changing Economy* (New York: Apex Press, 1991); Richard Kazis and Richard H. Grossman, *Fear at Work: Job Blackmail, Labor and the Environment* (Philadelphia: New Society Publishers, 1991).

4. Report of the Task Force on Environment, "Our Children's World. Steelworkers and the Environment," in United Steelworkers of America, *Report of the Committee on Future Directions of the Union*, 25th Constitutional Convention, Toronto, Canada, August 27-31, 1990.

5. The term "industry" here includes manufacturing, mining, transportation, and electric utilities. Manufacturing's share declined from 26 to 21 percent between 1960 and 1988. See OECD, *Historical Statistics 1960-1988*. Changes within the industrial sector from OECD, *The State of the Environment* (Paris, 1991).

6. *Economic Report of the President* (Washington, D.C.: U.S. Government Printing Office (GPO), 1989).

7. Barry Commoner, *The Poverty of Power* (New York: Bantam Books, 1976).

8. U.S. Department of Labor, Bureau of Labor Statistics (BLS), "Multifactor Productivity in U.S. Manufacturing and in 20 Manufacturing Industries, 1949-1986," unpublished database, April 1989.

9. Environmental Protection Agency (EPA), Office of Air Quality Planning and Standards, *National Air Pollutant Emission Estimates 1940-1989*, EPA-450/4-91-004 (Research Triangle Park, NC, March 1991); Chemical Manufacturers Association, *U.S. Chemical Industry Statistical Handbook 1990* (Washington, D.C.: November 1990). Although patterns of industrialization vary from country to country, the same basic picture arises outside the United States as well. See OECD, *The State of the Environment*, and Wolfgang Benkert and Martin Gornig, "Umweltschutz, Wirtschaftsstruktur und Arbeitsmarkt in Nordrhein-Westfalen," in Joke Frerichs et al. (eds.), *Jahrbuch Arbeit und Technik in Nordrhein-Westfalen 1988* (Bonn: Verlag Neue Gesellschaft, 1988). Sources for Table 1: Worldwatch Institute, compiled and calculated from U.S. Department of Commerce, Bureau of the Census, *1987 Census of Manufactures* and *1987 Census of Mineral Industries* (Washington, D.C.: U.S. Government Printing Office, 1990); U.S. Department of

Energy, Energy Information Administration (EIA), *Manufacturing Energy Consumption Survey: Consumption of Energy 1988* (Washington, D.C.: GPO, May 1991).

10. Share of energy and chemical industry employment calculated from "Energy Workers Worldwide," *Global Warming Watch*, Vol. 1, No. 1, 1990, and from International Labour Office (ILO), *Yearbook of Labour Statistics 1989-90* (Geneva, 1990). Refining industry from Keith Schneider, "Petrochemical Disasters Raise Alarm in Industry," *New York Times*, June 19, 1991. Coal industry from U.S. Department of Energy, Energy Information Administration (EIA), *Coal Production 1988* (Washington, D.C.: GPO, 1989), and from U.S. Department of Commerce, Bureau of the Census, *Statistical Abstract of the United States 1990* (Washington, D.C.: GPO, 1990). Coal employment forecast from ICF Resources Inc., "Comparison of the Economic Impacts of the Acid Rain Provisions of the Senate Bill (S. 1630) and the House Bill (H.R. 1630)," prepared for the EPA, Fairfax, Virginia, July 1990. Comparable European data are found in "Environment Statistics," Theme 8, Series C (Statistical Office of the European Communities (Eurostat)), 1989.

11. Wykle et al., *Worker Empowerment in a Changing Economy*.

12. For a more detailed critique of the pollution control approach, see Christian Leipert, *Die Heimlichen Kosten des Fortschritts. Wie Umweltzerstörung das Wirtschaftswachstum Fördert* (Frankfurt: Fischer Verlag, 1989), and Barry Commoner, *Making Peace with the Planet* (New York: Pantheon Books, 1990).

13. Ken Geiser, "The Greening of Industry. Making the Transition to a Sustainable Economy," *Technology Review*, August/September 1991; Amal Kumar Naj, "Some Companies Cut Pollution by Altering Production Methods," *Wall Street Journal*, December 24, 1990; Scott McMurray, "Chemical Firms Find that it Pays to Reduce Pollution at Source," *Wall Street Journal*, June 11, 1991.

14. Electroplating and metalfinishing examples from Valjean McLenighan, *Sustainable Manufacturing. Saving Jobs, Saving the Environment* (Chicago: Center for Neighborhood Technology, 1990). Electronics industry from Andrew Pollack, "Moving Fast to Protect Ozone Layer," *New York Times*, May 15, 1991. UNIDO furnishes additional examples in electroplating, waste-paper processing, printed circuit-board manufacturing, corrosion protection, textile printing, and other areas. United Nations Industrial Development Organization (UNIDO), *Industry and Development. Global Report 1990/91* (Vienna, 1990).

15. John E. Young, *Discarding the Throwaway Society*, Worldwatch Paper No. 101 (Washington, D.C.: Worldwatch Institute, January 1991). Energy use in car manufacturing calculated from Mary C. Holcomb et al., *Transportation Energy Data Book: Edition 9* (Oak Ridge, Tenn.: Oak Ridge National Laboratory, 1987).

16. Packaging share of paper production from Sandra Postel and John C. Ryan, "Reforming Forestry," in Lester R. Brown et al., *State of the World 1991* (New York: W.W. Norton, 1991). Packaging share of plastics from Anita Glazer Sadun et al., *Breaking Down the Degradable Plastics Scam*, Center for the Biology of Natural Systems (CBNS), Queens College, City University of New York, report prepared for Greenpeace, 1990. Highly indi-

vidualistic societies harbor a strong reluctance against proscribing the consumption of almost any product. Indeed, even the growth of "green consumerism" is an indication that alternative consumption rather than (selective) non-consumption attracts the most attention. For a discussion of related questions, see Alan Durning, "Asking How Much is Enough," in Brown et al., *State of the World 1991*.

17. Management Information Services Inc. (MISI), "Simulation of the Economic Impact of Pollution Abatement and Control Investment: Methodology, Data Base, and Detailed Estimates," Washington, D.C., May 1986; Geiser, "The Greening of Industry"; Ben Good, *Industry and the Environment: A Strategic Overview* (London: Centre for Exploitation of Science and Technology, 1990). In only a few cases do preventive expenditures account for a substantially higher share. To reduce air pollution, the U.S. refining, leather, primary metals, and paper industries devoted 54, 47, 40, and 37 percent, respectively, of their 1988 environment-related capital spending on changes in production technologies. U.S. Department of Commerce, Bureau of the Census, *Manufacturers' Pollution Abatement Capital Expenditures and Operating Costs. Final Report for 1988* (Washington, D.C.: GPO, September 1990).

18. The $171.5 billion figure understates the full scope of outlays because it excludes business spending to operate and maintain control equipment. The countries included are Britain, Canada, Denmark, France, Italy, Japan, Netherlands, Sweden, United States, and western Germany. See Gerhard Voss, "Umweltschutzausgaben im Internationalen Vergleich," *iw-Trends* (Köln: Institut der Deutschen Wirtschaft), Vol. 16, No. 3 (1989). 1972 to 1989 U.S. spending from MISI, "Economic and Employment Benefits of Investments in Environmental Protection," Washington, D.C., 1986, and from MISI, "PABCO Expenditures," unpublished draft, May 1990. Projection to 2000 from EPA, *Environmental Investments: The Cost of a Clean Environment. Report of the Administrator of the EPA to the Congress of the United States* (Washington, D.C., November 1990).

19. Asia estimate from Mark Magnier, "Market Abroad for Pollution Control Beckons," *Journal of Commerce*, December 8, 1989. South Korea from Joint Publications Research Service, "Ministry to spend $12 Billion to Clean Environment," *JPRS Report: Environmental Issues*, JPRS-TEN-91-003, February 5, 1991 (Washington, D.C.: National Technical Information Service, 1991). Taiwan from "Taiwan May End Use, Production of CFCs Ahead of World Schedule, Official Says," *International Environment Reporter*, May 8, 1991.

20. Current range of estimates from Magnier, "Market Abroad for Pollution Control Beckons," and from Michael E. Porter, "America's Green Strategy," *Scientific American*, April 1991. Projected spending from "£140 Billion Pollution Control Market Exists in the U.K., Industry Group Says," *International Environment Reporter*, February 13, 1991, and from Thomas Watterson, "Pollution Control Provides Investment Possibilities for the '90s," *Washington Post*, April 22, 1991. West German expenditures from Statistisches Bundesamt and Wissenschaftszentrum Berlin für Sozialforschung, "Aktualisierte Ergebnisse zum Anlagevermögen und zu Ausgaben für Umweltschutz 1975-1988," Wiesbaden, Germany, May 8, 1989, Table 8, and from Jürgen Blazejczak and Dietmar Edler, "Beschäftigungswirkungen von Umweltschutzmaßnahmen," *Wirtschaftsdienst*, No. IV, 1991. Other European countries from Directorate-General Employment, Industrial Relations and Social Affairs, Commission of the European Communities, *Employment in Europe 1990*

(Luxembourg: Office for Official Publications of the European Communities, 1990).

21. Hilary F. French, *Green Revolutions: Environmental Reconstruction in Eastern Europe and the Soviet Union*, Worldwatch Paper No. 99 (Washington, D.C.: Worldwatch Institute, November 1990). East Germany from "IFO-Studie: Die Rolle der Umweltschutz-Industrie bei der Sanierung der Neuen Bundesländer," *Ökologische Briefe*, February 20, 1991.

22. "1992" - *The Environment Dimension*, Report of the Task Force on the Environment and the Internal Market (Bonn: Economica Verlag, 1990); ILO, *Employment and Training Implications of Environmental Policies in Europe* (Geneva, 1989); Porter, "America's Green Strategy".

23. OECD, *Environment and Economics*, Results of the International Conference on Environment and Economics, June 18-21, 1984 (Paris, 1984), for possibility of cost increases. See UNIDO, *Industry and Development*, for a discussion of ways costs can be reduced. The U.S. oil and steel industries provide interesting examples of overdrawn cost estimates. In 1971, the U.S. oil industry argued that a phaseout of lead from gasoline would cost $7 billion a year. By 1990, with 99 percent of the phaseout accomplished, actual costs turned out to be only in the range of $150 million to $500 million. William G. Rosenberg, letter to the editor, *Science*, March 29, 1991. Similarly, in 1987, the EPA put the cost for the steel industry to control air pollutants from coke ovens at $4 billion. The agency's current estimate runs to $250-450 million. Keith Mason, "Looking Ahead: The Economic Impact," *EPA Journal*, January/February 1991.

24. Current and projected share of GDP from EPA, *Environmental Investments*. Dutch plans from William K. Stevens, "2% of G.N.P. Spent by U.S. on Cleanup," *New York Times*, December 23, 1990. Share of total U.S. plant and equipment expenditures from Gary Rutledge and Nikolaos A. Stergioulas, "Plant and Equipment Expenditures by Business for Pollution Abatement, 1987 and Planned 1988," *Survey of Current Business*, November 1988. Individual industries in the United States from MISI, "Simulation of the Economic Impact of Pollution Abatement and Control Investment: Methodology, Data Base, and Detailed Estimates," and in western Germany from Statistisches Bundesamt, Fachserie 19, Reihe 3, *Investitionen für Umweltschutz im Produzierenden Gewerbe 1988* (Stuttgart: Metzler-Poeschel, May 1991).

25. Kazis and Grossman, *Fear at Work*. On the question of technology-forcing versus technology-conservatism, see Marc H. Ross and Robert H. Socolow, "Fulfilling the Promise of Environmental Technology," *Issues in Science and Technology*, Spring 1991, and Porter, "America's Green Strategy." IFO-Institut from Lutz Wicke et al., "Entlastung des Arbeitsmarktes durch Umweltschutz?," *Mitteilungen aus der Arbeitsmarkt- und Berufsforschung*, No. 1, 1987. West German automation investments from Hans Christoph Binswanger et al., *Arbeit ohne Umweltzerstörung. Strategien für eine Neue Wirtschaftspolitik* (Frankfurt: Fischer Verlag, August 1988).

26. ILO, *Environment and the World of Work*, Report of the Director-General (Geneva, 1990); ILO, *Employment and Training Implications of Environmental Policies in Europe*.

27. Between 1979 and 1984, over 11.4 million jobs were lost due to plant closings. The EPA

figure also does not account for any rehiring of laid-off workers by the same or other companies, which apparently is substantial. See Kazis and Grossman, *Fear at Work.* OCAW findings from Wykle et al., *Worker Empowerment in a Changing Economy.*

28. National Coal Association from "NCA Looks at Coal's Multiplier Effects," *The Energy Daily,* August 20, 1990. ICF Resources Inc., "Comparison of the Economic Impacts of the Acid Rain Provisions of the Senate Bill (S.1630) and the House Bill (H.R.1630)." For considerations regarding electricity rates, see Mason, "Looking Ahead: The Economic Impact." R.M. Wendling and R.H. Bezdek, "Acid Rain Abatement Legislation—Costs and Benefits," *Omega,* Vol. 17, No. 3, 1989. The acid rain bills analyzed were HR.4567 and S.2203.

29. Methodological problems, and the absence of a standard definition of the pollution control sector, make it difficult to arrive at any precise measurement of pollution control-related employment. By most conventions, the sector includes such activities as air and water pollution control, sewage systems, and solid waste disposal (i.e., landfilling and incineration). It encompasses regulatory, administrative, consulting, engineering, construction, and equipment-manufacturing and operating activities. Most attempts to quantify the number of jobs have focused on the direct, short-term employment effects. U.S. employment estimates from MISI, "Numbers of PABCO Jobs Created in 1988," unpublished draft, Washington, D.C., May 1990. French job estimates from OECD, *Environment and Economics.* German data from Rolf-Ulrich Sprenger, *Beschäftigungswirkungen der Umweltpolitik—Eine Nachfrageorientierte Untersuchung,* Berichte des Umweltbundesamtes No. 4/89 (Berlin: Erich Schmidt Verlag, 1989), and from Rolf-Ulrich Sprenger, "Keine Beschäftigungspolitische Wende durch Umweltpolitik," *ifo-Schnelldienst,* No. 15, 1989. Share of total national employment in France and West Germany from ILO, *Employment and Training Implications of Environmental Policies in Europe.* For additional spending proposals in Germany and the Netherlands, see Gerd Oelsner, "Arbeit und Umwelt," in Norbert W. Kunz (ed.), *Ökologie und Sozialismus* (Köln: Bund Verlag, 1985), and Federatie Nederlandse Vakbonden and Landelijk Milieu Overleg, *Investeren in het Milieu* (Amsterdam, September 1987).

30. Benkert and Gornig, "Umweltschutz, Wirtschaftsstruktur und Arbeitsmarkt in Nordrhein-Westfalen."

31. MISI, *Economic and Employment Benefits of Investments in Environmental Protection,* Washington, D.C., 1986; Wendling and Bezdek, "Acid Rain Abatement Legislation—Costs and Benefits." Matthew L. Wald, "A New Geography for the Coal Industry," *New York Times,* November 25, 1990; ICF Resources Inc., "Comparison of the Economic Impacts of the Acid Rain Provisions of the Senate Bill (S.1630) and the House Bill (H.R.1630)." In 1988, U.S. average labor productivity in coal mining was 3.6 short tons per miner per hour. However, in Appalachia, the figure was 2.4, in the Midwest 3.5, and in the West 11.0, reaching as high as 18.8 in Wyoming and 19.6 in Montana. EIA, *Coal Production 1988,* Table 28.

32. ILO, *Environment and the World of Work.*

33. Christopher Flavin, *Slowing Global Warming: A Worldwide Strategy,* Worldwatch Paper No. 91 (Washington, D.C.: Worldwatch Institute, October 1989); Hilary F. French, *Clearing the Air: A Global Agenda,* Worldwatch Paper No. 94 (Washington, D.C.: Worldwatch Institute,

January 1990); Christopher Flavin and Alan B. Durning, *Building on Success: The Age of Energy Efficiency*, Worldwatch Paper No. 82 (Washington, D.C.: Worldwatch Institute, March 1988).

34. Capital requirements from Statement of Leonard S. Rodberg before the Subcommittee on Energy Conservation and Power, Committee on Energy and Commerce, U.S. House of Representatives, June 28, 1983. Christopher Flavin and Nicholas Lenssen, *Beyond the Petroleum Age: Designing a Solar Economy*, Worldwatch Paper No. 100 (Washington, D.C.: Worldwatch Institute, December 1990). Conclusions of German studies are reported in Binswanger et al., *Arbeit ohne Umweltzerstörung*.

35. Oregon data from Skip Laitner, Economic Research Associates, Eugene, Oregon, "Designing Energy Strategies to Incorporate External Costs into Public Policy: Where LES is More," paper presented to the National Regulatory Research Institute's Annual Conference, Columbus, Ohio, September 1988.

36. Steve Colt, University of Alaska, Anchorage, "Income and Employment Impacts of Alaska's Low-Income Weatherization Program," ISER Working Paper 89.2, prepared for Second Annual Rural Energy Conference, Anchorage, October 12, 1989.

37. Holger M. Eisl et al., *Investing in the Future: An Economic Analysis of the New York State Weatherization Assistance Program*, CBNS, Final Report, Prepared for New York State Department of State, Division of Economic Opportunity, April 5, 1991.

38. Worldwatch calculations, based on Eisl et al., *Investing in the Future*.

39. Economic Research Associates, "The Impact of the Northwest Energy Code upon the Idaho Economy," final report submitted to the Advisory Committee of the Association of Idaho Cities Economic Impact of Energy Project, September 30, 1990.

40. Leonard Rodberg, *Employment Impact of the Solar Transition*, a study prepared for the use of the Joint Economic Committee, Congress of the United States (Washington, D.C.: GPO, 1979).

41. Employment Research Associates, *Biomass Resources: Generating Jobs and Energy*, report prepared for the Great Lakes Regional Biomass Energy Program, Council of Great Lakes Governors, Lansing, Michigan, November 1985. The biomass sources assessed included alcohol fuel, energy from wood and from municipal waste, recovery of landfill methane gas, and recovery of methane produced at wastewater treatment plants.

42. The technologies included were residential building insulation, district heating, heat exchangers, heat pumps, domestic solar hot-water systems, and biogas plants. Given considerable methodological problems that the authors themselves point to, the results should only be seen as indicating the order of magnitude of job effects. See Commission of the European Communities, *Employment Effects of Energy Conservation Investments in EC Countries*, study prepared by Olaf Hohmeyer, et al., Fraunhofer Institute for Systems and Innovation Research (Luxembourg: Office for Official Publications of the European Communities, 1985).

43. H. Craig Petersen, "Sector-Specific Output and Employment Impacts of a Solar Space

and Water Heating Industry," Utah State University, Logan, Utah, December 1977.

44. Rodberg, *Employment Impact of the Solar Transition*; Statement of Leonard S. Rodberg before the Subcommittee on Energy Conservation and Power. Solar collectors which circulate liquids as a heat transfer medium require relatively more plumbing skills in installation, while air circulating systems rely more on duct-work and represent a better opportunity for sheet metal workers. See Petersen, "Sector-Specific Output and Employment Impacts of a Solar Space and Water Heating Industry."

45. A Minnesota study found that a dollar spent on petroleum products creates a demand for $1.49 of goods and services in the national economy, but only $0.64 in the state economy because the state relies on imported oil. A dollar spent on renewables, by contrast, has a net economic effect of $2.33-$2.92, because of higher local supplies. See Richard R. Lancaster, "Economic Impact of Alternative Energy Development in Minnesota," a report to the Legislative Commission on Minnesota Resources, Minnesota Department of Energy, Planning and Development, Energy Division, June 1983. For petroleum exporters' dependence on oil revenues, see Michael G. Renner, "Stabilizing the World Oil Market," *OPEC Review*, Spring 1988.

46. Solar employment from Statement of Leonard S. Rodberg. Lack of R&D support from Michael G. Renner, "Hot Air on Global Warming," *World Watch*, May/June 1990. *Photovoltaic Insider Report*, June 1991; Cynthia Pollock Shea, *Renewable Energy: Today's Contribution, Tomorrow's Promise*, Worldwatch Paper No. 81 (Washington, D.C.: Worldwatch Institute, January 1988; Christopher Flavin and Rick Piltz, *Sustainable Energy* (Washington, D.C.: Renew America, 1989).

47. Michael Renner, *Rethinking the Role of the Automobile*, Worldwatch Paper No. 84 (Washington, D.C.: Worldwatch Institute, June 1988); Marcia Lowe, *Alternatives to the Automobile: Transport for Livable Cities*, Worldwatch Paper No. 98 (Washington, D.C.: Worldwatch Institute, October 1990); Helmut Holzapfel et al., *Autoverkehr 2000: Wege zu einem Ökologisch und Sozial Verträglichen Straßenverkehr* (Karlsruhe, Germany: Verlag C.F. Müller, Schriftenreihe Alternative Konzepte No. 51, 1985); "Die 'Neue Bahn' Fährt noch mit dem 'Alten Denken'," *Ökologische Briefe*, No. 23, June 5, 1991.

48. Improved fuel economy does not imply any fundamental job effects in the motor vehicle industry itself. Still, to the extent that car manufacturers improve fuel efficiency by incorporating more light-weight plastic and aluminum components instead of steel, indirect employment shifts occur among supplier companies. The motor vehicle industry consumes a large share of the total volume of these materials produced every year. Between 1977 and 1989, the amount of steel per car manufactured in the United States declined by 22 percent, while plastics and aluminum grew by 34 and 60 percent, respectively. Motor Vehicles Manufacturers Association (MVMA), *Facts and Figures '90* (Detroit, Mich.: 1990). Worldwide, automotive demand for aluminum is expected to quadruple by the year 2000. "Vorfahrt für Aluminium im Autobau," *Süddeutsche Zeitung*, June 1/2, 1991.

49. "Automobile Workers Worldwide," *Global Warming Watch*, Vol. 1, No. 2/3, October 1990/January 1991; MVMA, *Facts and Figures '90*; Markus Hesse and Rainer Lucas, *Die*

Beschäftigungspolitische Bedeutung der Verkehrswirtschaft in Nordrhein-Westfalen, Forschungsprojekt im Auftrag des Instituts für Landes- und Stadtentwicklungsforschung (Berlin/Wuppertal: Institut für Ökologische Wirtschaftsforschung, 1990).

50. Hesse and Lucas, *Die Beschäftigungspolitische Bedeutung der Verkehrswirtschaft in Nordrhein-Westfalen*. East German railway jobs from "Wettbewerbsnachteile der Bundesbahn Vermindern Chancen einer Ökologischen Trendwende in der Verkehrspolitik," *Ökologische Briefe*, No. 24, June 12, 1991. Personnel shortage and overtime from Rainer Graichen, "Das Öffentliche Transportunternehmen Deutsche Bundesbahn als Instrument Beschäftigungssichernder Verkehrs- und Umweltpolitik," *WSI Mitteilungen*, No. 6, 1988.

51. Hesse and Lucas, *Die Beschäftigungspolitische Bedeutung der Verkehrswirtschaft in Nordrhein-Westfalen*; Markus Hesse and Rainer Lucas, *Verkehrswende. Ökologische und Soziale Orientierungen für die Verkehrswirtschaft*, Schriftenreihe des IÖW 39/90 (Berlin and Wuppertal: Institut für Ökologische Wirtschaftsforschung, 1990).

52. Hesse and Lucas, *Die Beschäftigungspolitische Bedeutung der Verkehrswirtschaft in Nordrhein-Westfalen*; Shawn Tully, "Comeback Ahead for Railroads," *Fortune*, June 17, 1991.

53. Hesse and Lucas, *Verkehrswende*.

54. German data include direct, indirect, and induced jobs, and are taken from Hesse and Lucas, *Verkehrswende*, from Graichen, "Das Öffentliche Transportunternehmen Deutsche Bundesbahn," and from Martin Junkernheinrich, "Beschäftigungswirksamkeit von Verkehrswegeinvestitionen. Eine Explorative Studie am Beispiel Nordrhein-Westfalen," unpublished manuscript, Institut für Ökologische Wirtschaftsforschung, Bochum, Germany, 1991.

55. Hesse and Lucas, *Die Beschäftigungspolitische Bedeutung der Verkehrswirtschaft in Nordrhein-Westfalen*; Hesse and Lucas, *Verkehrswende*. The developmental and production-related know-how of car manufacturers can easily be applied to chassis construction for light rail vehicles, for example. See Hinrich Krey, "Denkbare Alternative Produktionsansätze in der Automobil industrie," in Die Grünen im Bundestag (eds.), *Welche Freiheit Brauchen Wir? Zur Psychology der AutoMobilen Gesellschaft* (Berlin: VAS, 1989). Comparison of highway and bike path construction from Junkernheinrich, "Beschäftigungswirksamkeit von Verkehrswegeinvestitionen."

56. Young, *Discarding the Throwaway Society*.

57. Jim Quigley, "Employment Impact of Recycling," *BioCycle*, March 1988. In 1986, 80 percent of the total U.S. municipal solid waste stream was landfilled, 10 percent incinerated, and 10 percent recycled. U.S. Congress, Office of Technology Assessment, *Facing America's Trash: What Next for Municipal Solid Waste?*, OTA-O-424 (Washington, D.C.: GPO, October 1989). Employment in primary aluminum industry from Bureau of the Census, *Statistical Abstract of the United States: 1990*, Table 1209.

58. The data are for a variety of facilities of different capacity. Recycling depots receive and process materials from drop-off centers and curbside programs, and rely on manual separation and labor-intensive processing. Materials Recovery Facilities are larger facilities with automated separation and processing technologies. All numbers are based on the assumption that capacities are fully utilized. Vermont and New York City data are a Worldwatch calculation based on Tellus Institute and Wehran Engineering, *Analysis of Solid Waste System Costs for the State of Vermont*, report submitted to the Vermont Interregional Solid Waste Management Committee, Boston, Massachusetts, and Burlington, Vermont, July 1990, and on Jim Meyer, Deputy Director, Policy Planning, New York City Department of Sanitation, personal communication, July 12, 1991.

59. Barry Commoner, "Why Dump Recycling?," op-ed, *New York Times*, May 29, 1991.

60. Quigley, "Employment Impact of Recycling." For energy savings from recycling aluminum cans and glass bottles, see Young, *Discarding the Throwaway Society*. West German study is cited in Rudolf Hickel, "Wirtschaften ohne Naturzerstörung—Strategien einer Ökologisch-ökonomischen Strukturpolitik," in Frerichs et al. (eds.), *Jahrbuch Arbeit und Technik in Nordrhein-Westfalen 1988*.

61. David S. Wilcove and Jeffrey T. Olson, The Wilderness Society, "Biological Diversity and Conservation of Ancient Forests of the Pacific Northwest," paper presented at the annual meeting of the American Association for the Advancement of Science, Washington, D.C., February 18, 1991; "Agency Urges Widespread Logging Curb to Aid Spotted Owl," *New York Times*, April 27, 1991; John Lancaster, "Environmentalists Hail Freeze on Timber Sales to Guard Owl," *Washington Post*, May 25, 1991.

62. Job loss claims by timber industry and Thomas report estimates from John Lancaster and Rick Atkinson, "Saving Owl May Cost 20,000 Jobs," *Washington Post*, September 7, 1990. Tom Hamilton et al., "Economic Effects of Implementing a Conservation Strategy for the Northern Spotted Owl," U.S. Department of Agriculture, Forest Service and U.S. Department of the Interior, Bureau of Land Management, Washington, D.C., May 1, 1990.

63. Northwest forest loss from Wilcove and Olson, "Biological Diversity and Conservation of Ancient Forests of the Pacific Northwest." Adams from "The Future of Forests," *The Economist*, June 22, 1991. Leveraged buyouts from John C. Ryan, "Wall Street Goes Wild," *World Watch*, November/December 1989.

64. Wilcove and Olson, "Biological Diversity and Conservation of Ancient Forests of the Pacific Northwest." Jeff DeBonis, "Timber Industry's Claims," *Journal of Forestry*, July 1989.

65. Export share and profitability from Catherine Caufield, "The Ancient Forest," *The New Yorker*, May 14, 1990. Olson from McLenighan, *Sustainable Manufacturing*. The Forest Service/BLM report identifies additional options to save or generate several thousands of jobs, including boosting the net wood supplies through greater harvesting efficiency, enhancing recreational or commercial fisheries, gathering needed ecological data, and monitoring of forests. See "Plan to Save Jobs Suppressed," *Inner Voice*, Summer 1991. Proponents of the "Forests Forever" initiative in California to ban clearcutting claim that 40,000 timber jobs could be gained by curtailing the export of unprocessed trees. Wykle et

al., *Worker Empowerment in a Changing Economy.*

66. Wilcove and Olson, "Biological Diversity and Conservation of Ancient Forests of the Pacific Northwest." DeBonis, "Timber Industry's Claims."

67. British Columbia actual job loss from Caufield, "The Ancient Forest." Hypothetical job loss and share of all jobs in British Columbia from "The Provincial Economic Impacts of a Supply Reduction in the B.C. Forest Sector," *Forest Planning Canada*, July/August 1991. Australia from "Prime Minister Proposes Legislation to Guarantee Industry's Access to Forests," *International Environment Reporter*, May 8, 1991.

68. For example, it has been estimated that some 1,500 jobs may be lost due to efforts to preserve the Tongass National Forest in Alaska. But the Forest Service subsidizes logging there to the tune of $40 million a year. This sum of money could be used to pay each logger income support during a transition period. See Wykle et al., *Worker Empowerment in a Changing Economy*. Bush administration position from Brad Knickerbocker, "An Endangered Human Species," *Christian Science Monitor*, June 6, 1991. Redwood program from Kazis and Grossman, *Fear at Work*.

69. Phyllis Cribby, "Working with a Union to Create Jobs and a Sustainable Economy," *Journal of Pesticide Reform*, Vol. 10, No. 3. Bill Resnick, "Proposal - A Feasibility Study and Resource Identification for Transforming Oregon's Forest Products Industry," Labor-Environmental Solidarity Network Research Committee, Eugene, Oregon, unpublished draft, 1991.

70. Resnick, "Proposal - A Feasibility Study and Resource Identification for Transforming Oregon's Forest Products Industry"; Elliott A. Norse, "What Good Are Ancient Forests?," *The Amicus Journal*, Winter 1990; "Ancient Forests of the Pacific Northwest," Fact Sheet, The Wilderness Society, Washington, D.C., undated.

71. Eric Mann, "Environmentalism in the Corporate Climate," *Tikkun*, March/April 1990; Wykle et al., *Worker Empowerment in a Changing Economy*. Right to call for an investigation from Kazis and Grossman, *Fear at Work*. The European Community has proposed the establishment of eco-audits, but watered them down after encountering industry opposition. Instead of a mandatory framework, the revised proposal would make companies' participation voluntary. At the same time, the current draft does not provide for the workforce to be consulted during an audit. See David Thomas, "Brussels Backs Down on 'Eco-Audit'," *Financial Times*, April 5, 1991, and "Öko-Audit: EG-Vorschlag für Betriebliche Umwelt-Kontrolle," *Ökologische Briefe*, No. 23, June 5, 1991. A number of agreements have recently been concluded in the German chemical industry that give worker representatives greater access to relevant information concerning their company's operations. See "IG Chemie-Papier-Keramik Schließt Umweltschutz-Betriebsvereinbarung bei den Leuna-Werken ab," *Arbeit und Ökologie*, No. 14, July 3, 1991.

72. Harley Shaken (ed.), *Work Transformed. Automation and Labor in the Computer Age* (New York: Holt, Rinehart, and Winston, 1984); David Noble, *Forces of Production: A Social History of Automation* (New York: Oxford University Press, 1986); Binswanger et al., *Arbeit ohne Umweltzerstörung*.

73. Arthur Braunschweig, "Energieabgabe und Rentenversicherung. Überlegungen und Berechnungen für die Bundesrepublik Deutschland," in Hans G. Nutzinger and Angelika Zahrnt (eds.), *Für eine Ökologische Steuerreform. Energiesteuern als Instrumente der Umweltpolitik* (Frankfurt: Fischer Verlag, March 1990).

74. Klaus Gretschmann and Helmut Voelzkow, "Die Quadratur des Kreises: Energieabgabe und Rentenversicherung," in Nutzinger and Zahrnt (eds.), *Für eine Ökologische Steuerreform*.

75. John Gever et al., *Beyond Oil* (Cambridge, Mass.: Ballinger, 1987).

76. Reduced retraining funds from Robert Reich, "Who Champions the Working Class?," op-ed, *New York Times*, May 26, 1991. Funds as share of GDP from Nancy J. Perry, "The Workers of the Future," *Fortune*, Special Issue: The New American Century, Spring/Summer 1991.

77. Wykle et al., *Worker Empowerment in a Changing Economy*.

78. Byrd and Wise amendments from Wykle et al., *Worker Empowerment in a Changing Economy*. Packwood and Gorton legislation from "Owl Ruling Seen Keeping Lumber Out of Market," *Journal of Commerce*, May 28, 1991.

79. The German unions in particular have been pushing for introduction of the 35-hour week as a means of job creation. See Gerhard Bosch, "From 40 to 35 Hours. Reduction and Flexibilisation of the Working Week in the Federal Republic of Germany," *International Labour Review*, Vol. 129, No. 5 (1990).

80. Lloyd Jeffry Dumas, *The Overburdened Economy* (Berkeley: University of California Press, 1986).

MICHAEL RENNER is a Senior Researcher with the Worldwatch Institute and coauthor of the Institute's *State of the World* reports. Prior to joining Worldwatch, he was a researcher at the World Policy Institute in New York and a Corliss Lamont Fellow in Economic Conversion at Columbia University. He holds degrees in international relations and political science from the Universities of Amsterdam and Konstanz, Germany.

THE WORLDWATCH PAPER SERIES

No. of
Copies

____ 57. **Nuclear Power: The Market Test** by Christopher Flavin.
____ 58. **Air Pollution, Acid Rain, and the Future of Forests** by Sandra Postel.
____ 60. **Soil Erosion: Quiet Crisis in the World Economy** by Lester R. Brown and Edward C. Wolf.
____ 61. **Electricity's Future: The Shift to Efficiency and Small-Scale Power** by Christopher Flavin.
____ 62. **Water: Rethinking Management in an Age of Scarcity** by Sandra Postel.
____ 63. **Energy Productivity: Key to Environmental Protection and Economic Progress** by William U. Chandler.
____ 65. **Reversing Africa's Decline** by Lester R. Brown and Edward C. Wolf.
____ 66. **World Oil: Coping With the Dangers of Success** by Christopher Flavin.
____ 67. **Conserving Water: The Untapped Alternative** by Sandra Postel.
____ 68. **Banishing Tobacco** by William U. Chandler.
____ 69. **Decommissioning: Nuclear Power's Missing Link** by Cynthia Pollock.
____ 70. **Electricity For A Developing World: New Directions** by Christopher Flavin.
____ 71. **Altering the Earth's Chemistry: Assessing the Risks** by Sandra Postel.
____ 73. **Beyond the Green Revolution: New Approaches for Third World Agriculture** by Edward C. Wolf.
____ 74. **Our Demographically Divided World** by Lester R. Brown and Jodi L. Jacobson.
____ 75. **Reassessing Nuclear Power: The Fallout From Chernobyl** by Christopher Flavin.
____ 76. **Mining Urban Wastes: The Potential for Recycling** by Cynthia Pollock.
____ 77. **The Future of Urbanization: Facing the Ecological and Economic Constraints** by Lester R. Brown and Jodi L. Jacobson.
____ 78. **On the Brink of Extinction: Conserving The Diversity of Life** by Edward C. Wolf.
____ 79. **Defusing the Toxics Threat: Controlling Pesticides and Industrial Waste** by Sandra Postel.
____ 80. **Planning the Global Family** by Jodi L. Jacobson.
____ 81. **Renewable Energy: Today's Contribution, Tomorrow's Promise** by Cynthia Pollock Shea.
____ 82. **Building on Success: The Age of Energy Efficiency** by Christopher Flavin and Alan B. Durning.
____ 83. **Reforesting the Earth** by Sandra Postel and Lori Heise.
____ 84. **Rethinking the Role of the Automobile** by Michael Renner.
____ 85. **The Changing World Food Prospect: The Nineties and Beyond** by Lester R. Brown.
____ 86. **Environmental Refugees: A Yardstick of Habitability** by Jodi L. Jacobson.
____ 87. **Protecting Life on Earth: Steps to Save the Ozone Layer** by Cynthia Pollock Shea.
____ 88. **Action at the Grassroots: Fighting Poverty and Environmental Decline** by Alan B. Durning.
____ 89. **National Security: The Economic and Environmental Dimensions** by Michael Renner.
____ 90. **The Bicycle: Vehicle for a Small Planet** by Marcia D. Lowe.

_____ 91. **Slowing Global Warming: A Worldwide Strategy** by Christopher Flavin.
_____ 92. **Poverty and the Environment: Reversing the Downward Spiral** by Alan B. Durning.
_____ 93. **Water for Agriculture: Facing the Limits** by Sandra Postel.
_____ 94. **Clearing the Air: A Global Agenda** by Hilary F. French.
_____ 95. **Apartheid's Environmental Toll** by Alan B. Durning.
_____ 96. **Swords Into Plowshares: Converting to a Peace Economy** by Michael Renner.
_____ 97. **The Global Politics of Abortion** by Jodi L. Jacobson.
_____ 98. **Alternatives to the Automobile: Transport for Livable Cities** by Marcia D. Lowe.
_____ 99. **Green Revolutions: Environmental Reconstruction in Eastern Europe and the Soviet Union** by Hilary F. French.
_____ 100. **Beyond the Petroleum Age: Designing a Solar Economy** by Christopher Flavin and Nicholas Lenssen.
_____ 101. **Discarding the Throwaway Society** by John E. Young.
_____ 102. **Women's Reproductive Health: The Silent Emergency** by Jodi L. Jacobson.
_____ 103. **Taking Stock: Animal Farming and the Environment** by Alan B. Durning and . Holly B. Brough
_____ 104. **Jobs in a Sustainable Economy** by Michael Renner

_____ **Total Copies**

☐ **Single Copy: $5.00**
☐ **Bulk Copies (any combination of titles)**
　　☐ 2–5: $4.00 each　　☐ 6–20: $3.00 each　　☐ 21 or more: $2.00 each

☐ **Membership in the Worldwatch Library: $25.00 (overseas airmail $40.00)**
The paperback edition of our 250- page "annual physical of the planet," *State of the World 1991,* plus all Worldwatch Papers released during the calendar year.

☐ **Subscription to *World Watch* Magazine: $15.00 (overseas airmail $30.00)**
Stay abreast of global environmental trends and issues with our award-winning, eminently readable bimonthly magazine.

No postage required on prepaid orders. Minimum $3 postage and handling charge on unpaid orders.

Make check payable to Worldwatch Institute
1776 Massachusetts Avenue, N.W., Washington, D.C. 20036-1904 USA

Enclosed is my check for U.S. $_____

_____
name　　　　　　　　　　　　　　　　　　　　　　　　**daytime phone #**

_____
address

_____
city　　　　　　　　　　　　　　　**state**　　　　　　**zip/country**